Pelican Books

Making the Break

Melanie Carew-Jones has been involved with the Women's Aid Federation for four years, the last two of which have been spent as the housing worker for the Federation. She is now on the support group of Wandsworth Women's Aid. She lives in south London and has a son.

Hester Watson has been actively concerned with women's issues for the past eight years and joined the Women's Aid Federation in 1978. Since then she has worked for two and a half years in her local refuge, been a national coordinator of the Women's Aid Federation (England) for a year and a member of the national housing group for three years. She has been involved in researching and presenting the views of the Federation on issues such as housing, welfare benefits and funding to the government, the Press and the public. During a six-month visit to America she contributed to newsletters and a book on the international Women's Aid movement. In 1982 she had a daughter.

Melanie Carew-Jones

and Hester Watson

MAKING THE BREAK

Drawings by Cath Jackson

Penguin Books

Penguin Books Ltd, Harmondsworth, Middlesex, England
Penguin Books, 40 West 23rd Street, New York, New York 10010, U.S.A.
Penguin Books Australia Ltd, Ringwood, Victoria, Australia
Penguin Books Canada Ltd, 2801 John Street, Markham, Ontario, Canada L3R 1B4
Penguin Books (N.Z.) Ltd, 182–190 Wairau Road, Auckland 10, New Zealand

First published 1985

Copyright © Melanie Carew-Jones and Hester Watson, 1985
All rights reserved

Made and printed in Great Britain by
Richard Clay (The Chaucer Press) Ltd,
Bungay, Suffolk
Filmset in 9 on 11½pt Monophoto Photina by
Northumberland Press Ltd, Gateshead

Except in the United States of America, this book is sold subject
to the condition that it shall not, by way of trade or otherwise, be lent,
re-sold, hired out, or otherwise circulated without the
publisher's prior consent in any form of binding or cover other than
that in which it is published and without a similar condition
including this condition being imposed on the subsequent purchaser

CONTENTS

PREFACE

What you read in this book may not actually happen in practice because legislation is interpreted in different ways by different people. In addition the law frequently changes, either through new Acts of Parliament or court decisions, and some of the information may therefore be out of date. To the best of our knowledge the information here is correct at the time of going to print, but you may have to get advice on the current situation.

We would like to thank the following for the help they gave in producing this book: WAFE legal group, WAFE access group, Scottish Women's Aid, Northern Ireland Women's Aid, Wandsworth Women's Aid group, Nors Jackson, Annette Leslie, Paula Smithe, Maggie Pether, Sheila Stocking, Najat Chaffee, Sarah Blandy, Gabi Charing, Nicky Wilde, Sue Grey, Johanna Dobson, Ann Jessup, Isabella Forshall, Frances Simmons, Fran Logan and the Wandsworth Legal Resource Project.

1. INTRODUCTION

This book is about choices – in particular, the choice to end a violent relationship. It is for all women who are in violent relationships, whether married or cohabiting, experiencing violence and/or abuse from a son, a father, or a man who does not live with you; and whether or not you have children. It is about decisions which have to be made about whether to leave home and find somewhere else to live, or to stay in the home, either with the man or after trying to force him to stay away by using the law. It has been written by women who have lived and worked in Women's Aid refuges, and we have written about the experiences we have had of leaving a home and a relationship, or of working with women who have done so. We want it to be a practical guide for all those women who are experiencing violence in their lives, in giving them the information they need to make decisions and to carry them out. Throughout the book we use the term violence as a general one, and by it we mean mental and sexual violence as well as assault or the threat of it.

We recognize that every woman's experience is different, but we want to give some idea of what can be involved both practically and emotionally. We have tried to be realistic about the limitations of the law, about how other people will react to you, about being alone with your children, and about financial independence; but we also want to show that these problems, though very real, are not insurmountable. With support from each other and advice from people who have experience in the areas of law you will be using, many women have taken such action and, although it is not easy, have built new lives.

The Women's Aid Federation (England) is a feminist organization which links most of the refuges in this country. To join the federation, a refuge group has to support the seven demands of the women's movement and the five aims of WAFE which are:

1. To provide temporary refuge, on request, for women and their children who have suffered mental or physical harassment.
2. To encourage the women to determine their own future and to help them to achieve this, whether it involves returning home or starting a new life elsewhere.
3. To recognize and care for the emotional and educational needs of the children involved.
4. To offer support, advice and help to any woman who asks for it whether or not she is a resident, and also to offer support and after-care to any woman or child who has left the refuge.
5. To educate and inform the public, the media, the police, the courts, social services, and other authorities, with respect to the battering of women, mindful of the fact that this is the result of the general position of women in our society.

There are also Women's Aid federations in Wales, Scotland and in Northern and Southern Ireland. There is a separate organization in each country, because not all the laws relating to divorce, housing, domestic violence and children are the same in each of these countries, and different circumstances may also affect what sort of help you are able to get. The legislation which we describe in the book applies mainly to Wales and England. Although the situation regarding housing in Scotland and social security in Scotland and Northern Ireland is the same as in England, much of the legislation is separate and quite different. We have pinpointed the main differences in Chapters 10 and 11, but women from these countries should contact their own federations for more detailed information.

There is now a growing movement to provide what might be called 'specialist' refuges. In Manchester, London and Sheffield there are refuges and resource centres run by and for Asian women. These refuges and centres can provide the sort of help which involves an understanding of Asian culture and, sometimes, another language. They will also be aware of complications that may arise as a result of marriage ceremonies and divorces performed in different countries, and of possible immigration problems. Women's Aid has recognized that Asian women have felt isolated, and therefore we support the setting up of refuges for Asian women. In recent years, many WAFE groups have tried to operate in an anti-racist way and have positively discriminated in favour of employing black women as paid workers, but there has been a recognition among some black women that there is a need to set up refuges run by and for black women. A group has also been set up recently for incest survivors, which is looking into the possibility of providing refuges for girls and young women who have experienced this form of sexual abuse and violence from men.

Throughout the book we shall be making reference to Women's Aid Refuges, not just as an option for temporary accommodation when you leave home, but also as a source of support and advice for any woman who is in a violent relationship. Not all women will want to go into a refuge and, of those that do, some may not be able to at their first attempt because there are simply not enough refuge spaces for all the women who need them. This is particularly true of metropolitan cities like London, Birmingham and Newcastle, and in a political and economic climate where many Women's Aid Groups are having their funding cut or withdrawn, the situation can only get worse.

If you go to a Women's Aid refuge, you will be sharing accommodation with women and children who have had experiences similar to your own. Many women have talked about the relief they felt in going to a refuge and being able to talk to other women who had been through the same sort of thing, and realizing that their relationship is not unique and is not their fault. On a practical level, a Women's Aid refuge offers a woman who wants to leave a violent partner an immediate safe place to go for herself and her children.

Much of this book is about the legally enforceable rights of a woman who wants to leave a violent man. The legislation that exists to help us in this situation has been hard won by campaigns involving the women's movement, housing agencies and sympathetic MPs, but unfortunately the spirit in which the laws were drafted has, to some extent,

been lost, either on their way through Parliament or in subsequent interpretations by the authorities. This means that there are limitations to the amount of use we can make of the legal rights that we have gained. In carrying out decisions about your future you will be using a combination of housing, matrimonial and children's law. Our experience has shown that it is often difficult for us to assert our rights under these laws and we have tried to point out the complications and difficulties that may have to be overcome in trying to enforce them. You will almost certainly need to get legal advice if you intend to use the law, so we describe where you can get help and how to get legal advice which is freely available if you cannot afford to pay for it, under the legal aid scheme. You will, in addition, have to make decisions which do not relate simply to legal rights, so we consider the question of financial independence and adapting to life as a single parent, as well as the areas covered by legislation.

Securing the future that you want will involve a series of decisions concerning such questions as where you will live, the future of your children and what legal action, if any, you want to take in order to secure your own and your children's safety. We try to give you the information you need in order to make those decisions, and how to cope when things do not turn out as expected, in which case there may be other options that you can try.

Two of your major concerns will be whether you should seek some form of legal protection from your partner, and whether to remain in your home or leave and get permanent or temporary accommodation elsewhere. Whatever your decision you are entitled to some money to live on. In Chapter 4 we describe the different sorts of benefits and who can claim them, and how to go about claiming, as well as possible complications and how to deal with them. It is likely that you will need to claim some sort of benefit even if you have a job, and you will have to decide whether you want to claim some money from your partner.

In our experience one of the many reasons which stop a woman leaving home is anxiety about where she can go. For this reason we go into the choices of temporary accommodation that are available. We look at bed-and-breakfast hotels, homeless persons hostels, short-life housing – whether independent or local authority – staying with friends and going to a refuge. We give some idea of the disadvantages and advantages of each option and try to be realistic about what it is like living in temporary accommodation. While you are away from home, you may decide to seek permanent accommodation elsewhere. Your most realistic option when you want to do this is to apply to the local authority for rehousing, either by making an application under the Housing (Homeless Persons) Act or by applying for a transfer from your former home if you already have council tenancy. In Chapter 3 we describe how to apply for council housing, who is entitled to it, the sorts of problems you may come up against and how to deal with them. We also go into the other options for permanent accommodation: housing associations, private renting, co-ops and buying.

Whether you remain at home or leave, you may want to seek legal protection. If you decide to do this, you can get a court order to prevent your partner molesting, assaulting or interfering with you in any way, called a non-molestation order, and you can get an exclusion order to exclude him from the home. You may decide you need both types of order. The different types of order and how you can get them are described in Chapter 5, where we also assess how effective each of them may be and go into the advantages of different laws you can use to get these court orders.

If you decide to stay in your home with your partner, you need to assess whether such an order will actually prevent him from being violent. A court order which excludes him from the home is only a temporary solution, and if you wish to stay there without him permanently, you can do this through divorce proceedings which we describe in Chapter 6. Your rights to the home if you are not married are quite different and will depend on who was the tenant.

Another major decision that you have to make is whether you want the children to live with you or not. If you do, it is better to take them with you when you leave or, if that is not possible, fetch them as soon as you can. Otherwise you can apply to the court for an order saying that you should have them. Chapter 6 tells you how to go about getting legal custody of your children, how access arrangements are made and how to get maintenance. We deal in this chapter with the process of the law, while in Chapter 7 we describe the complications which can arise if your husband contests your right to custody of the children, or the local authority decides to take them into care. We also look at what rights children have when their parents split up and what facilities there are for helping you to cope when you have settled down to living as a one-parent family. The prospect of becoming a one-parent family often discourages women from finally making the break from a violent partner, so in Chapter 8 we look positively at ways you can adapt to life as a single parent and how it is possible to live alone with your children very successfully.

We set out, in each chapter, the problems, complications, and set-backs that you might face when trying to use the legislation and, wherever possible, how to deal with them. There are some additional complications which you may have to consider as soon as you decide that you want to end the relationship. If you are an immigrant and you are not absolutely sure that you have a right to stay in the UK independently of your husband, you will need expert advice on your immigration status. We describe in Chapter 9 the situations in which you might have problems with the immigration authorities. Your right to live in this country can be affected by a change in your circumstances such as leaving your husband, or changes made by the government in the immigration regulations. It is best to check out your position with advice agencies or a solicitor who is experienced with this type of law, before taking any other legal action, claiming benefit, or going to the housing department.

When you begin to make decisions about your future and that of your children, you need, first, to think about what you want, and then to consider all your options in the light of your particular circumstances. You can get help from Women's Aid, advice agencies and solicitors, who can tell you what your options are and how effective each of them might be for you. Whether you are able to enforce your statutory rights will depend on which part of the country you are in and who you approach for help. When you apply to the local authority for permanent housing, for example, your chances of success will depend on which local authority you approach and how sympathetic they are. They may not help if you are not covered by the precise provisions of the Housing (Homeless Persons) Act, or they may have a general policy of helping women who have had to leave home because of violence. Similarly, if you decide to seek legal protection, you may not get the type of court order that you need if the judge presiding at the court is unsympathetic to your case. Once you have a court order, it will not be effective if your partner chooses to ignore it and the police are inefficient and uninterested in enforcing it, or if the court does nothing to punish him for breaking it. You may also have to take into account the effects that one decision will have on your other options. If you decide to seek protection through the courts, for example, this may affect your application to the council for permanent housing, because they might consider that a court order removes the risk of violence, so they will not accept responsibility for rehousing you.

When deciding whether to apply for custody of your children, you may wish to consider whether your partner will apply for access if you start any legal proceedings. We describe some of the problems associated with access in Chapter 6 and how courts are likely to grant access even though it can lead to further trouble for you. Your partner may discover where you are living if he has access to the children and it will mean that you have to remain in some sort of contact with him. You may decide, instead, to take the children with you to live elsewhere and not to take any legal steps to formalize your separation.

We have tried in this book to set out all the different options and information to help you decide what to do. However, if you are not successful with one course of action, you may be able to get what you want using another, so don't give up. With help, your chances of success are increased: contact a local organization like Women's Aid, and a law centre, community centre or solicitor who knows what the local courts, judges and housing departments are like, in order to get an idea of what to expect. In some areas you may find it more difficult to do this as there are fewer sources of help available, and unfortunately this tends to coincide with a greater reluctance of the courts to grant domestic violence injunctions with powers of arrest, and of local authorities to offer suitable alternative permanent accommodation. If you live in an isolated rural area it might be worth seeking help in the nearest large town, or moving out of the area, even temporarily, to a place where you can find advice and help in sorting out your future.

Because of the way that society individualizes our relationships within the family, we are made to feel that any breakdown or problem in our relationship must be due to something we have done wrong. If a husband, boyfriend, father or brother is violent, we must in some way have provoked such a response. Women's Aid is of the opinion that the problem stems from men and their behaviour, and that women should not be blamed for the problem of male violence. It is hard to keep sight of this when many of the individuals and agencies that you may turn to for help reinforce the idea that yours is an individual problem to which you have somehow contributed. It is these attitudes which you may come up against when you seek the aid of statutory agencies and the legal system in your attempt to leave a violent man. We hope that this book will prepare you for this, warn of some of the pitfalls involved and equip you for making the break successfully. We at Women's Aid feel that it is a measure of the way that society views violence against women in the home and the relative positions of women and men that this book has to be about women uprooting themselves from their homes and having to build new lives, when it is men who are the problem.

2. LEAVING HOME

PLANNING TO LEAVE

Leaving home is a big step for anyone to take, but particularly if it follows the break-up of a relationship with your partner. You may have been thinking about leaving for a long time, or you may suddenly have come to the decision. If possible, it is better to plan how you are going to leave, so that you have things you need with you and so that you know where to go for help.

If you have time, remember to take with you – apart from anything else you may need – your child-benefit book and some clothes. Some women who plan their departure have a bag already packed. Clearly, it is not always possible to plan ahead, particularly if you have to leave after a violent or threatening incident. It should be possible to get help at any time of the day or night. Most women who leave in an emergency at night go to the police, by whom they may be referred to social services or a refuge. Alternatively, they may go temporarily to friends.

You may decide to leave home temporarily rather than permanently. It is possible to go for a short time, with the intention of returning home, either by going back to live with the man, or after having excluded him from the home. Decisions such as these will probably take a lot of thought and you may want to spend some time making them. If you are in a refuge or with friends, you can take your time, but if you are in council accommodation, the council may pressurize you to make decisions quickly. In any event, it is better to decide within quite a short time what action to take, so that you can start working towards a solution, which could take months to achieve. It is important to remember, too, that you can change your mind at any time. Do not be pushed into making decisions you aren't happy about.

Some solicitors may advise you not to leave home at all, even when the man is being violent. They may say that it jeopardizes your chance of getting the home if there is a property settlement in court. This is often not true, particularly when there has been violence, and you should never remain at home just for this reason. If you leave, you can arrange getting your home back later. It is not worth enduring more violence because of the advice of a solicitor.

Once you have left and found somewhere to stay for the night, you can begin to sort out getting some money. This can always be done the next day, so do not worry if you have to leave without any cash. You will also have to start thinking about your housing, the future of the children, schools, and possible legal protection. It is a good idea to get help with sorting out these problems: get in touch with the local Women's Aid group and they will advise you, even if you are not living in a refuge (see Appendix I for contact numbers and addresses). Alternatively, try the Citizens Advice Bureau (CAB), social services, housing aid centre or any independent advice agency, who should be able to help. If you cannot find anyone to help in your area, ring up the WAFE office in London or Women's Aid in Scotland or Wales and they will give advice over the telephone and put you in touch with the nearest Women's Aid group. It is also a good idea to talk to a doctor, health visitor or social worker as soon as possible so that someone else knows about the problems you have had.

It is better to take the children with you when you leave, if you want them to live with you in the future. If you become involved in a custody case, your chances of winning may be affected if your partner argues that you 'abandoned' the children. If you are forced to leave the children behind, it is possible to collect them the next day, or a few days later. If your partner will not let you take the children, you could arrange to pick them up from school, or while he is out. (See Chapter 7.)

WHERE YOU GET HELP

Where you go for help depends on the time of day you need it and what services you have in your area. If you leave at night you can go to the police or straight to Women's Aid, if you already know how to contact them. Only some local authorities have an emergency number, which you can get either by telephoning the town hall or from the police. The telephone exchange will give you the number of the town hall and there will either be someone there to answer your call or an answering machine that gives you the emergency number. In the daytime you can go to the housing department of the local council, to social services or to any advice agency. All of these should help you to get temporary accommodation and it is they who should do the work in finding it. You may, however, find some of them unhelpful, and you may not get results at your first attempt. It may mean several phone calls or visits, but do not give up; if one agency does not help, then try another. Do not be put off – you will find somewhere in the end. Impress upon them that you cannot return home because you are in danger. Make sure they take you seriously, otherwise they may just tell you to go home.

POLICE

The police will often refer women to refuges or contact emergency social services, who should then organize accommodation, at least for the night, before arranging something more long-term. However, if the police are called to your home when your partner is being violent, you cannot always rely upon them to help you. Your partner may be able to talk himself out of the situation, and if he insists that you are hysterical, he may be believed.

If you are badly hurt the police may take you to hospital, but do not assume that they will find you somewhere else to go. Ask someone in the hospital for help; there may be a hospital social worker who will help you.

THE HOUSING DEPARTMENT

The housing department has a duty to provide emergency temporary accommodation if you cannot return home because of the risk of violence. Do not let them tell you to go home. If they persist in refusing to help you, contact Women's Aid or another advice agency.

REFUGES

The police, housing department, social services and advice agencies can all refer women to refuges, or if you know the telephone number you can contact the refuge yourself to ask for advice and/or accommodation. If you ring the WAFE office in London, we will put you in touch with your nearest refuge. This could mean making a few telephone calls because of the need for security and shortage of refuge space, but you will not be turned away.

WHERE YOU CAN GO AND STAY

When you leave home, temporary accommodation can be found while you think about what to do and arrange either going back home or getting permanent accommodation elsewhere. Your three main options will be:
a) staying with friends or relatives;
b) finding a refuge;
c) approaching the council for temporary accommodation (to meet your immediate needs).
The first has to be arranged by yourself, and the other two can be arranged either by yourself or by any of the above agencies.

STAYING WITH FRIENDS

You may go straight to the home of a friend or relative to stay there while you sort out what to do next. When you go to friends, you must consider, firstly, whether you will be safe at an address that your partner probably knows and, secondly, how it will affect your long-term plans. If you decide to apply to the council for permanent rehousing, the length of time you spend staying with friends could be relevant. You should go immediately to the homeless persons' unit of the council to register as homeless and, if necessary, persuade them to let you stay with your friends rather than go into temporary accommodation. If you stay with your friends long enough to get settled, before approaching the council, they may not then consider you to be homeless. In some areas you may be told, after only one night, that you are not homeless if you have been with a relative or friend. Even though you may be very overcrowded, this only warrants going on to the ordinary housing waiting-list which could mean years of waiting. If you are told you are not homeless because you have a home with your friends, you may have to become homeless from that address before being accepted by the council for rehousing. In practice, this means your friends issuing you with a notice to quit. Some councils will insist that a court order is obtained before they will accept anyone in this situation as homeless. The council may send one or two officers to the property to see if relations between you and your friends have really broken down irretrievably, and they may try to get your friends to retract the notice to quit. You should present a united and antagonistic front, and prepare the reasons why the relationship broke down very carefully so that you cannot then be declared 'intentionally homeless'.

GOING TO A REFUGE

A refuge is a place where women and their children can stay when they are escaping from the violence of the man they live with. There are over two hundred refuges in Britain run by different organizations: local authorities, the Church, Samaritans or privately, in addition to the federation of refuges in England, Scotland, Wales and Northern Ireland. Refuges all over the country vary greatly in, for example, how they are run, the standard of accommodation, facilities and size. Each organization operates differently: some refuges are run as hostels with a live-in warden; some have no workers and are run by the women living in the house with support from local women. Some are purpose-built with individual flats for each woman and her children. All refuges will offer emergency accommodation and there will be other women there who will help you to sort out what to do.

There are 142 Women's Aid refuges in England, twenty-six in Wales, twenty-six in Scotland and four in Northern Ireland, and although they do vary a great deal, they operate on similar principles. There are no conditions attached to being accepted into a refuge: you may or may not have children, you may or may not come from that area. Refuges will accept a woman who is being mentally, physically or sexually abused by a man, whether he be father, husband, son, boyfriend or brother, and whether or not she lives with the man. One of the most important things a refuge can offer is the chance to meet other women who have had experiences similar to yours. You will discover that you are not the only woman to live with a violent man, and the other women will understand when you tell them what you have gone through. Living with other women gives you the opportunity to exchange experiences and information, and to offer support to women who will support you. In general, the condition of most refuges is poor and although some Women's Aid groups have been able to secure funding, so that they can improve the property, most have not, and standards of decoration and furnishings will not be high. There is almost always overcrowding, and you will have to share kitchen and living-room facilities with other women and children. However, as far as possible, you will be given your own room for yourself and your children.

Women's Aid refuges are run on the principle of self-help, and after you've had a few days to settle in, you will be encouraged to take part in the running of the house. The refuge may have paid or volunteer workers who visit the refuge regularly and can provide information and practical help. They, together with the other women in the house, can offer support, but basically you will be encouraged to start doing things for yourself once you have settled in. You'll probably get used to phoning up and hassling DHSS and council officials for yourself fairly quickly, but other women will be able to help you gain the confidence to do this. The refuge will be able to put you in touch with solicitors who have more than the usual amount of experience with divorce, separation, custody and access work, and will also have contacts with local authorities, housing associations, doctors, etc., which you can use.

In many refuges there will be some sort of provision for children: there may be a play-room and equipment; there may be a paid worker who will take them out or run a playgroup. Some refuges run their own play schemes in the school holidays. The refuge will have good links with local schools and can arrange for your children to get places quite quickly; so, although interruption of their schooling is a worry if you are thinking of leaving home, it is something that can be sorted out very quickly.

'I lived in a refuge for nine months before I was rehoused by the local council. I had my own bedroom which I shared with my three sons aged seven, three and one. There were three other families living in the same house and we shared the kitchen, bathroom and front room. At times it was hard; you didn't get much peace and quiet, there was always someone going and as soon as they went, someone else came, yet there were a lot of good times. You had a laugh with the other women in the house about the things that had happened, and it was so nice to talk to people who had been through the same thing themselves.

When I first got there I felt unsure of myself – didn't know what to do; I felt nervous as well in a funny sort of way. I don't know why, because everyone was nice enough and as soon as you got there they made you a cup of tea and gave the boys a drink. They then showed me my room and left me to settle the boys down. After that, I came downstairs and soon we were talking like I had known them all my life.

The next day it seemed like it was all go – I was given appointments for the social security, and then to see the solicitor as I wanted to get an injunction against him. After that, I had to sort out my eldest son's schooling, then get on to the council to see if they would give me a transfer. Some hope. At first it seems never-ending, then you sit down in the evenings and talk to the other women and in some way it helps you through. Also there are workers there who help you: if it wasn't for the other women plus the workers I wonder if I would ever have got through it.

The boys started to play up, which other women had said they would do and it is only a phase they go through. I thought it would never end but it does. The eldest one became really cheeky, the middle one became very spiteful towards other children, which you feel bad about, especially when he goes up to some child and bites him for no reason at all, and you feel so helpless. What can you do about it? But they do get out of it. I know at times I never thought he would, but he did. Then the baby who was always a happy little soul turned into a moaner. I even started thinking, "Is it worth it? I may as well just go back home." But there was always someone to talk to about it and the next day it would be all different.

As I said, I was there nine months, which is a long time, but it was worth waiting for: I now have my own place. I go back to the refuge every week and see them all – have a chat.

That is one thing when you have lived in a refuge: you meet lots of new people and you are always welcome to go back there for a chat and a cup of tea. I am glad I stuck it out. Just to do what I want to do has made it all worth while.'

The other women in the refuge, both the workers and the women who live there, will be able to give advice on what you need to know about claiming benefit, your different housing options, and legal proceedings. You will be given all the information necessary to make a decision about which procedures you need to go through. No one will pressurize you and you will not have to make decisions immediately. You may need time to think things over – this may be all you want from the refuge.

Some women come to refuges over and over again when they have had enough at home. Most refuges are willing to accept women back more than once, if they return to live with their husband or boyfriend. So, if you have left home before and gone back, do not be put off leaving again if you have to.

Arriving at the Refuge

When you first arrive at the refuge, you will probably feel alone and scared, but maybe relieved, too. There will be someone to talk to when you get there, a cup of tea, and someone to see to the children and help them settle in.

If you are expecting to go to a refuge, it's a good idea to take some sheets and towels with you, but don't worry if you can't. If you arrive at the refuge with nothing, you can probably borrow clothes and food for the first couple of days. The most urgent thing that needs to be sorted out is money: you can do this either by going straight to the social security office or by making an appointment with them. You should get a payment on the day of the appointment. Someone in the refuge will tell you the phone number of the DHSS and what to do. Another urgent need is for your clothes, if you have had to leave with nothing. If the refuge has transport and your home is quite near by, women from the refuge will be able to go with you to your house to collect your things; if they don't have transport, you will have to get a taxi or ask a friend to collect your things for you. If you do go back, it is important to take the police with you, and it's a good idea to take a friend for moral support. This applies whether you are in a refuge or not. The police will only take you seriously if you explain that you wish to go to your home to collect your personal belongings and that your partner is very violent, and you think there may be a 'breach of the peace'. You may have to wait a long time but the police will usually send someone with you.

Leaving the Refuge

When you eventually move into a new home, the refuge can sometimes help with transport and with furniture. People often donate furniture to refuges and, if it can be stored, it can be given to women moving into new houses who may have nothing other than what social security provides.

Because the refuge is such a close-knit community, many women remain in contact with the group when they leave and will visit and help out, and may join the support group, so the refuge becomes a long-term commitment. Some women feel very reluctant to leave the refuge because it is secure and full of other women to give support; the transition to living alone with the children is a difficult one and the refuge group will help as much as it can.

APPROACHING THE COUNCIL

To do this you must go to the homeless persons' unit of the local authority. If you go to the town hall, they will tell you where this is. If it's night-time and you contact any of the agencies mentioned above, they should tell you to approach the homeless persons' unit the following day (unless you go to a refuge, in which case you can wait until you are ready).

If you go straight to the council without an appointment, you will probably have to wait for a while before they will see you. If possible, take a friend with you and ask her to come into the interview room with you for moral support. You should first say that you can't go back to your home because you are in danger of violence from the man you live with. (If you're not living with the man who is threatening you, the council won't help you with rehousing – see sections on legal protection and housing transfers for action you can take.) The homelessness officer will then ask for some details about yourself and your children, and will probably ask what your long-term plans are. But you don't have to go into this; just say that you haven't decided yet. The officers will probably suggest that you go to a solicitor and may try to refer you to one that the local authority uses. Do not go to this solicitor unless you know that she is good and sympathetic. The implication behind asking you to see a solicitor is that the council expects you to sort out your housing problem yourself, by asserting your rights to your home through the courts. This means that you are expected to get a court order to exclude your partner from the home – often without first being told what the other options are. Local authorities will often ask women to go to court for injunctions, and this is for one or both of two reasons. Either they want you to get the court to remove your partner from the home and then return to live there yourself, or they want you to prove that there has been violence. It's just as well to say that you are intending to see a solicitor; even if you don't want to or can't get an injunction against your partner, you may want to start divorce, custody or maintenance proceedings.

As well as asking you questions, the homeless persons' unit makes its own investigations into your circumstances. The extent of these will vary according to local policy, but generally involves getting in touch with social services and contacting local authorities in areas where you lived previously. They may also contact your doctor or neighbours, and in a few areas the homeless persons' unit has been known to visit the man to ask if he would have his wife back!

If you do not have children the local authority does not have a duty to provide temporary accommodation but should offer you 'advice and assistance' in finding your own accommodation. This can vary in different areas. Some local authorities will offer women without children temporary accommodation and will offer permanent rehousing too. They may provide a list of local hotels but offer no assistance in finding a space, or may refer women to refuges. Some authorities will merely turn women away, telling them to go back home, or advise them to get a court order or to stay with friends. If you approach the council at night, through social services, for example, they may possibly find you somewhere to stay overnight (if they can't refer you to a refuge), but it is unlikely to be for longer than one night. If the council does not give you temporary accommodation, then try to find somewhere to stay temporarily, rather than go back home. Contact Women's Aid or find out from an advice centre or the housing aid centre whether there is any possibility of permanent rehousing from the council either through the waiting-list or through special schemes for single people.

If you do have children, or are pregnant, old or disabled, the council should offer you temporary accommodation immediately while they carry out their investigations and consider whether they are liable to house you permanently. Women who have children also often get refused temporary accommodation, but in doing this the council is acting unlawfully and you should get legal advice from a solicitor, advice or law centre, CAB or Women's Aid. It might be a good idea to get support from your social worker, if you have one you can trust, who can help you in your dealings with the council.

Some areas are worse than others about providing temporary accommodation. If you are turned away by the homeless persons' unit – who may just tell you to return home or to go to a solicitor – don't give up. You can contact Shelter National Housing Aid Trust for advice, if there is no advice agency in your area. Contact Women's Aid to see if there are any refuges in your area; or you can even go to a refuge away from your home town. You need not necessarily apply to your own local council for accommodation. If you think it would be dangerous to apply in the same area, you can go elsewhere and apply to the council there for housing. Although you have the right to apply for housing anywhere, this may make it harder to get permanent housing, but the authority where you apply should provide temporary accommodation initially. If possible, however, try to find out from Women's Aid or a local advice agency what the council is like in the area that you want to go to – you may find yourself under one of the most unsympathetic authorities just through bad luck.

The sort of help you get from the council may vary between none at all and an offer of permanent housing. There *are* statutory duties and it is important to know what these are if you are going to have to argue with a homelessness officer (this is another reason for taking someone with you). Some authorities do not fulfil these duties, and it is very hard to argue when you have just left home and are all alone. Don't always accept what they say without question. Go elsewhere for help and support so that you can approach the council again feeling more confident. If they are acting unlawfully, the only way to force them to change their minds is by going to court, which is a very long process, so it is better if you can persuade them to help you.

Storage of Furniture

If the local authority accepts a responsibility to rehouse you under the Housing (Homeless Persons) Act, then they also have a duty to assist you to protect your property (furniture and personal possessions). If they have reason to believe that your furniture may be damaged or lost, then they should, according to the Code of Guidance to the Act, take 'reasonable steps to prevent the loss or to prevent the damage'. This usually means that they will put your possessions into storage while you wait to be rehoused. They can make a charge for this, however, which will vary in different areas. In practice, many local authorities do not offer to store furniture, but it is always worth asking. If they refuse, you may be able to get social security to pay for storage costs.

Temporary Accommodation

If you are offered temporary accommodation by the council, it could be any sort of property. You may be referred to a refuge: refuge spaces are available to all women who have been mentally or physically abused by men, whether they have children or not. You may be referred to a hostel or to a reception centre, you may be offered a short-life property (although this is not likely to happen immediately), or you may be placed in a bed-and-breakfast hotel. You should always ask to be given temporary accommodation other than a bed-and-breakfast if you have children, but in most places this will not be possible – some local authorities do not have their own homeless family accommodation. Temporary accommodation should be used as somewhere for you to stay while investigations are being carried out in connection with your application for permanent housing or while you sort out returning home. Even when the council has made a decision to rehouse you permanently, you may find yourself staying in temporary accommodation for some time. This may be because they are waiting for a suitable property to become available or it may be the result of a punitive policy that homeless people have to spend a certain amount of time in temporary accommodation before being made permanent offers. Examples of such a policy exist in Bristol and Runcorn where women have to wait until six months after all rent arrears are cleared before they are offered permanent housing.

If, as a result of their investigations, the council decides not to offer you permanent accommodation because they think you are not homeless (and can go back home) or not in 'priority need' (you have no children and are not 'vulnerable'), then they can ask you to leave the accommodation they have provided immediately. If you are in a bed-and-breakfast and they have been paying part or all of the cost, they will just stop paying it. It is then up to you whether you continue to do so. If they decide that you have made yourself homeless intentionally, then they have a duty, if you have children, to provide accommodation for enough time for you to find alternative accommodation. The time for this will vary: in areas where there is very little housing you may get two months, but it is generally twenty-eight days. See Chapter 3 on permanent housing for an explanation of how the council can refuse.

Refuge

If you get referred to a refuge by the council, you will be in the same position in the refuge as if you'd gone there yourself. It may be a local authority refuge, but refuges are usually independent of the council. You can make an application for permanent housing, if you wish, from the refuge.

Hostels and Reception Centres

Most local authorities have property which is specifically for homeless people to stay in while investigations are being carried out. The standard of property varies enormously; you may have to share a room with your children, and the standard of cleanliness may be low. Some allow self-catering, while others have no such facilities and may even expect you to be out of the room most of the day. The number of homeless families far exceeds the amount of hostel space, and as a result homeless persons' units are generally very crowded. The problems caused by such overcrowding can make them uncomfortable and intimidating places, particularly for a woman on her own with children.

Bed-and-Breakfasts

Even where there are local authority hostels for the homeless, the council will almost certainly have to use bed-and-breakfasts as well, to cope with the numbers. Some councils have a policy *not* to use bed-and-breakfasts as they are very unsatisfactory, particularly for women with children. Most bed-and-breakfast hotels are lonely, isolated places, although they do vary in standards quite a lot as regards cleanliness, breakfasts, where there are cooking facilities, the number of people sharing a bathroom, etc. In some cases accommodation has been so bad that women have called in the Press to expose what sort of conditions they are forced to live in. Do not hesitate to use this method of securing decent accommodation if you think it might work. Many hotels do not allow cooking in rooms, but you may be able to have an electric kettle. Some do not allow the residents to remain in their rooms during the day, which may mean you have to wander the streets all day before being allowed back into the hotel. If at all possible, ask about these things before you go there. The homelessness officer will probably just give you an address and a letter for the owner of the hotel, but try to insist you go somewhere suitable for children. A disadvantage of bed-and-breakfasts is that they could be anywhere, not necessarily in the area where you are applying for housing. If you have friends or relatives who you want to spend the days with, you may have problems with travel and may be rather cut off. You could also be moved about from one place to another, which is very disorienting, particularly for the children.

Bed-and-breakfast hotels vary a lot, from the best, where some cooking facilities are available and there is a landlady who likes children, to the worst, where the food is appalling and the landlord is openly racist. However, if you are placed in one of these hotels by local authorities, you may have no other options. You should attempt to make your stay as short as possible by telephoning the council every day to ask either for their decision on whether you are homeless or when you can expect to get an offer of a tenancy. If conditions are so bad that you want to complain, then get in touch with a local councillor, or if you just need support, get in touch with your nearest Women's Aid group. Try to find out if there is a day-centre anywhere near by or a nursery where the children could go in the daytime. Social services should give you this information. There is probably nothing that can make your stay in a bed-and-breakfast pleasant, but do not give up and go home. If you are accepted as homeless your stay can only be temporary.

Short-life Housing

Short-life housing is property which is waiting to be converted into new permanent flats or houses, and is therefore usually in quite bad repair and may have been empty for some time.

Some local authorities use short-life housing for homeless families before offering them permanent accommodation. It is very unusual for a homeless family to be given a short-life property straight away but you may be offered one after a period in bed-and-breakfasts, if it is likely to be a long time before you are offered anything permanent. Some authorities use short-life housing as a sort of penance for people who have rent arrears, and may not offer anything permanent until the arrears are paid. It is difficult to argue about this, as the council has fulfilled its duty in providing accommodation, but you can argue that it is not 'suitable'; and if you are being asked to pay off arrears, check that they are in fact your responsibility before agreeing to pay. The standard of short-life housing varies, obviously, but if you are offered a short-life tenancy which you consider to be unfit for habitation, then get legal advice about your position before you refuse to accept the offer. It is one of the disadvantages of being offered short-life property that it is often in bad condition, and the council are unlikely to make any repairs if the property is due to be converted. It will usually be unfurnished property and you will need to spend some money to make it comfortable. If you are eligible for single payments from the DHSS, you can apply for furniture grants, but this means that you cannot claim for another grant when you move into your permanent home.

The advantage of short-life housing as temporary accommodation is that you are self-sufficient and can settle into a new routine more quickly than if you were in a bed-and-breakfast, for instance; you are likely to be living on your own with your children. Housing associations also have short-life property which they sometimes let out temporarily and can, though rarely, offer in an emergency. This will be more fully explained in the section on housing associations (pp. 53–5).

If you are granted a temporary licence for a property after the local authority has accepted a responsibility to rehouse you, then after twelve months that licence may become a secure tenancy. So if you are in a short-life property for twelve months, get legal advice regarding your tenancy status.

3. FINDING A PERMANENT HOME

There are many different options to consider in finding a permanent home and there are many different types of housing and different types of tenancy: council, housing association, private rented, ownership, and squatting. However, not all women have access to all of the different types, and it depends on whether you have money, whether you have any children, your age, your state of health, and whether the man who was violent was actually living with you.

Your options are limited by whether or not you are married and what sort of place you lived in before you left home; for instance, a woman who owned her own home has different options from a woman who had a council tenancy. This chapter describes each of these options, who can get them and who cannot. It is about finding a new home, so if you want to return to your own home with the man removed, see Chapter 5 which describes how to use the law to exclude your partner.

IF YOU OWN YOUR HOME

If you are married, then the future of the matrimonial home depends largely upon the divorce court, which will decide on a property settlement. If you want to return home, it is possible that the court will give the house to you and the children, or you may be allowed to live in the matrimonial home until the children are all over sixteen and out of full-time education. This means that when the children are old enough, the house is to be sold and the proceeds divided between you and your husband. Although this sort of arrangement may seem agreeable at first, there is a danger that when the house is sold you will suddenly find yourself homeless, perhaps with not enough money to buy another home, no longer in priority need and therefore not eligible for assistance from the council. This is not a permanent solution, so discuss it carefully with your solicitor.

Alternatively, you and your husband may agree, or the court may force you, to sell the house immediately and divide the proceeds between you; then you can either buy a house somewhere else or try other options for housing. The council will not rehouse you if you can afford to buy a house for yourself. Proceedings such as these take a very long time and you will either have to wait in a refuge or other temporary accommodation, or return home with a court order until the house is sold. If you have approached the council for help, they might rehouse you before the matrimonial home is sold, if they have evidence that you will not get enough money to buy another house. This is quite rare, but worth trying, and you should get your solicitor to write to the council to explain why you will not get much money from the property settlement. Even if the house is in your husband's name, you have rights to the home and you can prevent him from selling or mortgaging it before the divorce by 'registering your interest in the land' (your husband can do the same if it is in your name). To find how to do this ask at your local CAB. You can find out whether the property is already registered by asking the mortgage company. If you want to do this, it is possible to do so without your husband finding out.

Women from owner-occupied property have the option, more often than other women, of buying their own home, but it means perhaps months of legal wrangling in the courts to get money out of the home. This can often be the most contentious issue in the divorce and can lead to further trouble from the man (which you should inform your solicitor about). Many women decide to leave their home and do not try to force the husband to sell. Some local authorities, however, if they are approached for help, will insist that you do try to force a sale; if you think you are putting yourself in danger, then do not agree. It is another example of how women are forced into the position of suffering the penalty of having married a violent man.

If you are not married you have no automatic right to the property unless it is in your name or jointly owned. When the home is in your name only, you can evict the man, as he has no permanent right to live there. If it is in joint names, you will probably have to go to court, unless you can agree on a settlement to divide the house, so it is best to consult a solicitor as soon as possible. If the house is in the man's name, it might be worth going to see a solicitor, as it is possible that a court could make an order for compensation, if you can prove that you have contributed to the mortgage, deposit, or cost of the house; but you will not be able to remain in the property permanently. (The council should then rehouse you, because you cannot assert any rights to the property.) If you do not wish to go back to the home and you are the sole or joint owner, you are in the same position as a married woman when trying to persuade the local authority to house you.

COUNCIL HOUSING

Everyone has a right to apply for council accommodation and to be interviewed by the homelessness unit, but this has no bearing on who may be accepted. You may either apply as homeless under the Housing (Homeless Persons) Act 1977, or you can join the ordinary waiting-list if you have somewhere to live already but want to move to council property. When you apply to the council and are accepted as homeless, they don't necessarily have a duty to provide you with accommodation, if by their giving you advice you are able to secure accommodation for yourself. The women least likely to be offered accommodation are either those who have no children or whose children are living elsewhere. In many areas, women in this situation will not be accepted for rehousing but just advised to return home or to find private accommodation. Women who have enough money to buy their own home will often be refused housing on these grounds but will be offered advice on how to obtain a mortgage. Some local authorities will themselves guarantee or grant a mortgage. If you are eligible for council housing you will usually get it, if you fulfil all the conditions, under the Housing (Homeless Persons) Act; otherwise, if you are already in council property, you can get a transfer from one tenancy to another. The ordinary waiting-list for applications is usually not relevant to women who have left home because of violence, as it takes so long to be offered a tenancy. In some areas, however, where there is a lot of available housing, the waiting-list is an option for women who have a place to stay temporarily until an offer is made, which could take as little as three months.

THE HOUSING (HOMELESS PERSONS) ACT

Under this law, the council has a duty to provide housing for anyone who

a) is homeless;
b) is in 'priority need';
c) is not intentionally homeless;
d) has a local connection.

It is also this law which says that the local authority should provide temporary accommodation for anyone applying as homeless until investigations into their circumstances are completed. Attached to the Act is a Code of Guidance which advises authorities on how to carry out their duties under the Act. This is quite sympathetic to women who have left home because of violence and even suggests to authorities that the fact that violence has not yet actually taken place does not mean that a woman is not in danger. However, this Code has no statutory effect. It has no legal force behind it and local authorities are within the law if, in practice, they just ignore it. If you are going to approach the council, it is still a good idea to know a little about what the Code says to back up your arguments; it may not make any difference to the decision, but it will show that you know what you are talking about. When you first apply to the council you will be interviewed by a homelessness officer who, depending on which council you are applying to, will be more or less sympathetic. She will take down your details and will then decide whether you fulfil the four conditions. Although these conditions seem to be quite straightforward, they rarely are; each local authority interprets the Act differently, which is why it is so important to know what the conditions mean and how they are likely to be interpreted.

HOMELESSNESS

The Act says that a person is homeless if she has no accommodation, if she has accommodation she cannot get into, if she has a mobile home and there is nowhere to put it, or if it is probable that occupation of the accommodation would lead to violence or threats of violence from another person living there and he is likely to carry out those threats. Women who leave home because of violence should, then, be accepted as homeless. The definition will usually cover violent sons and fathers as well as husbands or boyfriends. The first problem concerns women

who have boyfriends or husbands who do not live with them but are still violent. If you are in this position, you will not be considered under the Housing (Homeless Persons) Act and you will probably not be given temporary accommodation. You should then apply for a transfer to another tenancy which could take a very long time. (See the section on transfers, pp. 48–53.)

Violence

The Code asks authorities to respond sympathetically in situations where violence has not yet occurred, but in practice most authorities will insist on some sort of evidence of physical violence before they will help. Some will accept the woman's word if she is in a refuge, but it is more common for them to ask for doctors' reports, police reports or statements from witnesses. In some cases they will ask you to get a court order, usually a non-molestation order, to prove that violence did actually occur and that you are serious about ending the relationship. You should not agree to this if you are too frightened or don't want to get one. The council should not force you. If you have been to your doctor or social worker, you can ask them to contact the homelessness unit to support your application. You will not always be asked to produce evidence, but if they insist, try to get a friend or someone from Women's Aid to back you up. When the local authority refuses to accept that there has been violence you may have to take further advice.

Local Authority Refusals

Some authorities will refuse to accept your application under the Housing (Homeless Persons) Act because you already have a tenancy or you own your home. The reaction in many authorities is that they will assist you to get back into your home by advising you to get an 'ouster' injunction to remove the man. They would then expect you to return home as they consider that you are no longer at risk from him. The problems of 'ouster' injunctions and their frequent ineffectiveness are described in Chapter 5 and you should always refuse to get one if you do not intend to go back or if you do not think it would prevent your husband or boyfriend from being violent. Be wary of entering into any 'deals' with the local authority about getting rid of the man in exchange for a new tenancy, because they could change their minds. It is unlawful for them to terminate the tenancy if the man is the tenant and they have no grounds for eviction. If you own your home, the council is more likely to expect you to wait until the property settlement has been finalized, so they can assess whether you can return to the matrimonial home or whether you can buy somewhere on your own before offering permanent rehousing. They may suggest that you wait in your home with the protection order while this is sorted out, they may offer temporary accommodation, or you can stay in a refuge. If they consider that you do not have enough money to buy a place and they accept that you cannot return home because of the risk of violence, they will offer you accommodation.

Another barrier put up by local authorities specifically affects women in refuges. This is when the authority refuses to accept women as homeless when they are staying in a refuge on the basis that they have somewhere to live. There has been more than one court case concerning this point and it has been legally determined that women in refuges are living in crisis accommodation and are therefore still homeless. This also applies to night shelters, hostels where you do not have access to your room during the day, and temporary hostels where you have no licence to occupy any part of the building. If the council refuses to accept you on these grounds and refuses to back down, you will have to get legal advice.

If possible, take someone with you from the refuge when you approach the council.

If You are Forced out of the Home by Your Boyfriend
If you are thrown out and the property is in your boyfriend's name only, you should be accepted as homeless by the council if you are not married. You have no legal rights to remain in the property and the council cannot lawfully tell you to return.

PRIORITY NEED

When you are accepted as homeless the council will then consider whether you are in 'priority need'. You will be in 'priority need' if
a) you have dependent children;
b) you are pregnant;
c) you are vulnerable – the definition of this will vary and is clarified below.

If you are not in priority need, then they have a duty to provide 'advice and assistance', which in practice often means nothing, but it can be advice on accommodation agencies or information on special schemes for single people that operate in the area.

Having Dependent Children
Although this may seem an indisputable fact, you may find that the council will not regard you as being in priority need if your children are in temporary care or if you do not have full costody.

The Act says that if your children are normally expected to live with you then you should be considered to be in priority need – if the council does not accept that you are, then you should get a letter from the children's social worker to give to the council, saying that they will live with you. If the future of the children is not finally sorted out, ask the social worker anyway. Too often women are told by the council that they will not be offered accommodation until they have the children with them, and social services will not let the children return to their mother until she has somewhere for them to live. Women's Aid will offer support to women who are caught in this trap and will tell social services that a woman can bring her children to the refuge if she requests it.

Until 1982 it was common practice for the local authorities to ask married women to get full custody before offering them permanent accommodation, which was to prove to the council that you were in priority need' and would remain so. They imagined that if they rehoused a woman in family-sized accommodation and she lost custody, they would be forced into providing two homes for one family. In 1982 there was a court case which established that women do not have to have full custody of their children in order to be considered in priority need: just having them with you is enough. However, in some areas authorities are still demanding that women get custody papers before they will offer permanent accommodation. If this happens, point out that they are breaking this legal precedent; you should not have to get custody and, if necessary, you should take legal advice. Some local authorities will ask unmarried women to get custody orders, which is totally unnecessary as unmarried women have automatic custody of their children. If you have staying access, the council do not have to take this into account when considering your application, or the size of the property they are likely to offer. (Staying access means that you have access to your children and they stay with you overnight.)

If You are Pregnant

Many local authorities are convinced that women will go to any lengths to get a council tenancy. To avoid unpleasant arguments it is better, if you are pregnant, to take a doctor's note to the interview certifying the fact, particularly if you have no other children, as this brings you into the category of priority need. The more extreme authorities will refuse to rehouse you until you are at least seven months pregnant, to avoid the possibility of your terminating the pregnancy after getting a flat. Once they have accepted you, they should not reverse that decision, even if your circumstances change.

'Vulnerable'

The Housing (Homeless Persons) Act says that if you are vulnerable as a result of old age, mental handicap, physical disability or any other special reason, you should be included in the priority groups. This is not a very clear definition and has often been abused by local authorities. It has been clarified slightly by a court decision in 1982 according to which vulnerable means 'less able to fend for oneself so that injury or detriment would result when a less vulnerable man [*sic*] would be able to cope without harmful effects'. If you apply for housing under this category, you need to have evidence from doctors, social workers, or a hospital that you should be considered vulnerable. It is not usual for women to be housed under this category unless they are old or severely handicapped, but if you have psychiatric, drink, or related problems, you should get help from social services or Women's Aid in applying. In the Code of Guidance it is suggested that childless battered women should be considered vulnerable, but it is very rare for women without children to get rehoused under this category. From a survey done in Women's Aid, we discovered that some areas did accept childless women, others only accepted them on to the ordinary waiting-list, and others would only accept them if there was another reason such as old age or physical or mental handicap. To convince an authority which is not sympathetic requires a lot of evidence and arguing. If you have a dependant who is vulnerable (for instance, an aged mother or a handicapped child) and who would normally live with you, then you should be considered to be in priority need; it does not have to be the applicant who is vulnerable.

INTENTIONAL HOMELESSNESS

If you are accepted as being homeless and in priority need, the local authority will next consider whether you made yourself homeless intentionally. If they think you have done something, or failed to do something, which has resulted in your losing your home, then you can be declared 'intentionally homeless' and refused permanent housing. You may be declared intentionally homeless if

a) you give up a tenancy;
b) you refuse advice and assistance from the council;
c) you refuse an offer of accommodation.

Giving up a Tenancy

In order to declare someone intentionally homeless, the council has to show that you did something which led to the loss of your home, that you understood all the relevant facts, and that it would be reasonable for you to stay in the accommodation. The Code of Guidance says that women who have left home because of violence should never be declared intentionally homeless; neither should a tenant who is evicted because of rent arrears or one who gives up a tenancy and moves in with relatives and is then asked to leave a few months later. Since the Housing (Homeless Persons) Act was introduced, the interpretation of what giving up a tenancy means seems to have widened, and more and more homeless people are refused help by the council on these grounds. Despite the Code of Guidance, this includes many battered women. A large number of local authorities will declare you intentionally homeless if you give up a tenancy before leaving home or if you gave it up before being offered another one. Many women do give up tenancies, which are in their own or joint names, because they are sure they will never go back and do not want to run up rent arrears. If you do this you run the risk of being declared intentionally homeless, even if you did not realize this would be the result of your action. It is wiser, therefore, not to give up a tenancy even if you intend moving far away, because it leaves you something to bargain with, and it is easier to pay off rent arrears than to shake off the label 'intentionally homeless'. If they threaten to take the tenancy away after you leave because you have abandoned the property, they have to take you to court to do so. Get legal advice.

The same dangers apply to women from private tenancies or owner-occupiers. Private tenants who give up their tenancy, or allow themselves to be evicted without a fight, may be declared intentionally homeless because they failed to defend the eviction order. Owner-occupiers may be held to be intentionally homeless if they sell their homes before the mortgage company forces them to.

Never give up a tenancy or rights to a property before taking advice on your housing options.

Refusing Advice and Assistance

The local authority may offer 'advice and assistance' to people who apply under the Housing (Homeless Persons) Act instead of providing permanent or temporary housing. What it means is that they will give you advice and assistance in finding accommodation for yourself. If you leave home because of violence and go to the council for help, you may be advised to go to a solicitor, get a court order to remove the man, and return home. This sort of advice and assistance is often offered to women without children, because the council does not have a responsibility to rehouse them. However, it is also offered to women who do have children and for whom the council does have a responsibility. They may tell you that in advising you to go to solicitor and get a court order, the council has fulfilled its duty towards you. They may find you a refuge or temporary accommodation until the court order is granted, but will not provide any permanent housing.

If you do not take this advice, and do not attempt to get a court order to remove your partner, the council may say that you are intentionally homeless, because you have refused their advice. Try to argue and tell them that it would not be safe, that injunctions are notoriously difficult to enforce and that you would be in danger of further violence. If the council makes its final decision, which you should get in writing from the homeless persons' unit, that you are intentionally homeless, then you should get legal advice. If you go to a solicitor, she may be able to get the council to alter their decision by telling them that you cannot go to court for an injunction, as you do not intend to return home. If this fails, your solicitor may threaten them with legal action on the basis that they have not fulfilled their duty under the Housing (Homeless Persons) Act. In some cases where the council has been threatened with legal action, they have reversed their decision, so it is worth threatening them with this even if you do not think you could face the whole legal process. There is no legal precedent to say whether the council is acting unlawfully or not, so be very wary of taking your case to court if you are not sure that you are going to win.

If you do accept their advice and return home with a court order, you will have to go back to the council with evidence that your partner has broken the order, before they will consider helping you further.

If you are too frightened to go to court to get an injunction and too scared to return home, do not let the council force you to do so. There is ample evidence to show that injunctions do not always work and you know best how much effect it is likely to have on your partner. More and more authorities are using the Domestic Violence Act to reduce their responsibilities towards battered women. Women in Southend, Canterbury and Suffolk Coastal District have been declared intentionally homeless for this reason. If you have problems like this then contact WAFE who will find you a place in a refuge and will give you advice.

Refusing an Offer

Local authorities differ as to how many offers of accommodation they will make once they have accepted you as homeless. Often you will get only one, which is likely to be in the worst of their housing stock. You will probably know in advance if you're going to get more than one offer – if you're not sure then ask the homelessness officer and check with an independent agency. Even where you will get more than one, weigh up carefully before you refuse a tenancy, as the next may be just as bad or worse. If you are going to get only one offer, it will be sent to you with a short threatening letter telling you that if you refuse it you will not be given another one and the council will have considered that it has fulfilled its duty towards you, and you will be regarded as intentionally homeless if you apply again. Some local authorities are more strict than others on this; some will mean it and some will back down if you argue enough. Do not refuse an offer until you know the council's policy or have checked whether you have legal grounds for rehousing.

The property the council offers you must be 'suitable and appropriate', which, of course, gives them quite a lot of discretion to interpret as they want. When making an offer, they should take into account things like medical reports, distance from special schools and, if you are getting away from a violent man, the distance from your previous home. A recent court case extended the definition of 'appropriate' to mean distance from employment and where the children go to school, so it may be possible to refuse an offer on the grounds that it is 'inappropriate'.

If the condition of the property is so bad that you cannot accept it, you will have to get support to back up your arguments from social workers, the local Women's Aid group, health visitors, environmental health officers and councillors, where possible.

LOCATION AND LOCAL CONNECTION

The last condition that homeless people must fulfil to be rehoused by a local authority is to have a local connection with the area. This can mean past residence, employment, or close relatives living in the area. If you don't have a local connection, then the authority may refer you to an area where you do have a connection. However, this condition should be waived for women who have left home because of violence. If you leave home and decide to go as far as possible away from home (and you have a right to apply for housing anywhere in the country) the authority that you first approach – the 'receiving' authority – should not tell you to go back to your original authority. The 'receiving' authority should interview you and, if you have children, offer you temporary accommodation while they make investigations into your circumstances. They will probably contact the council where you lived before to check that you did actually live there and whether you are at risk of violence there. If they find you are homeless, in priority need, and not intentionally homeless, then they should accept you for rehousing because you are at risk in the area with which you do have a connection. In practice, this very rarely happens so smoothly. Very few authorities will rehouse women who come from outside their area, even if they are escaping from a violent man. Some will refuse even to interview you if they know you have come from outside the area and will tell you to approach your own council. This is not lawful; the receiving authority has a duty to carry out investigations and, if necessary, contact other authorities. If you are told to apply elsewhere, get support from other agencies in the area, or go straight to a solicitor or advice agency. Once you have been offered temporary accommodation by the receiving authority, they may attempt to refer you elsewhere for permanent rehousing. This may even happen when you do have a local connection with the area. It might not be that you have lived there in the past: a local connection can mean having close relatives living in the area.

The two main methods by which an authority may try to avoid responsibility towards you are:

1. The council will advise you to get an injunction to exclude the man from the house. This advice is based on the argument that if there is a court order, then you are no longer at risk in your home area and therefore can be referred back there. The discussion about injunctions is described in full in this book and you should use all those arguments and refuse to return if you think you will not be safe.

2. The authority will negotiate with the original authority and get them to commit themselves to rehousing you in an area within that authority away from where you lived previously. Once the original authority has agreed to rehouse you, the receiving authority considers it has fulfilled its duty towards you. If you think this might be what the council will do, then get in touch with the original authority yourself (or get someone from an advice agency or Women's Aid to do it for you) and try to persuade their homelessness unit not to accept the referral, on the grounds that you would not be safe. The receiving authority must rehouse you themselves if the original authority refuses. You may not succeed in persuading the original authority not to accept the referral, in which case you must argue on the grounds that you would be bound to meet up with the man using the same bus routes, shopping centre and pubs (the children may be at the same school, and visit the same friends, and he could find you with this information), and that, therefore, you would not be safe and the offer is not suitable. You may be asked to prove that you would not be safe anywhere near your husband or boyfriend, but for many women providing such proof is nearly impossible. If you agree to take out a non-molestation order to prove that violence did occur, the receiving authority may use that against you later to say that you are protected from further violence by that order.

Very many women do get turned away if they approach a different authority from their own. If possible, when you reach a new area, try to get in touch with the nearest Women's Aid group, as they will have had experience of this problem and will give you advice and support.

This is a very complicated area of the Housing (Homeless Persons) Act and its abuse; you should get advice if possible on how to avoid being referred back home.

It is advisable to consider which local authority you want to apply to before you leave home because your own authority is unlikely to house you outside their area. Some authorities do refuse to accept referrals of women who previously lived in their area and have left home because of violence. This does not always work to your advantage if you actually want to return to where you have friends and family. In this instance, you would have to argue that you would be safe, as you have the protection of these friends and family.

IF THE COUNCIL REFUSES TO ACCEPT YOU FOR REHOUSING

What the council does depends on why they have refused to accept responsibility for rehousing you. They are supposed to supply a written notice of their decision and their reasons, which should be available for you to collect at the council offices.

If you are not homeless, then they have no duty towards you.

If you are not in priority need, then they have a duty to provide you with 'advice and assistance' in finding accommodation, which could be anything from a list of hostels and accommodation agencies which deal with single people, to information on special schemes for single people. Some local authorities do have 'hard to let' schemes which they let to single people, and there may be housing associations that deal exclusively with single people, or a housing co-op which houses single people in the area. You can find out about this from the housing aid centre or a local advice agency.

If you are declared intentionally homeless, the council has a duty to advise you on how to find alternative accommodation, and to continue to provide temporary accommodation for as long as it should take, on average, to find somewhere else. This time limit for providing temporary accommodation can vary in different areas, according to the extent of the housing shortage, from twenty-eight days to three months. The authority has no obligation towards you if you have not found anywhere in that time – they can just evict you from the temporary accommodation. If you are declared intentionally homeless by the local authority, they will not usually accept another application for housing from you until you become homeless from secure accommodation again. This means that if you are declared intentionally homeless, then find yourself temporary accommodation and apply to the council when you have to leave, you will probably still be regarded as intentionally homeless. If you are refused for this reason by one authority, you cannot apply immediately to another. When the new authority finds out that you have already been declared intentionally homeless, they will probably come to the same decision.

If you have children and have left home because of violence or threats of violence and the council refuses to offer you accommodation, the chances are that you have fallen through one of the loopholes in the Housing (Homeless Persons) Act. There is no formal way of appealing, but if you think they have made their decision unfairly, then you should get in touch with an independent advice agency either locally or in the nearest large town, or by contacting WAFE or Shelter National Housing Trust. There are CABs all over the country, and there are many more advice and law centres, though mostly in large towns. Social services can sometimes help, but do not rely on it. A sympathetic councillor may be able to help by pushing your case. This is not always successful, but is worth trying. Councillors often hold 'surgeries' in their local area where they talk to people who have had problems. You can contact your councillor through the town hall. All these agencies can help put pressure on the council to reverse their decision, but if they are adamant, your only option is to take legal action: take the council to court to force them to change their decision. Your first step should be to go to a solicitor to see what your legal position is. If you decide to fight the council in court, the first thing your solicitor can do is to threaten court action, which may make them back down. If they do not, it could lead to court appearances and a very long wait while all the procedures are gone through. You must be prepared for this, as it is intimidating, takes a long time, and may set a precedent for other women. Only take your case this far if you are sure that you are going to win.

WHAT SORT OF HOUSING?

If you are accepted for rehousing, the council will accept responsibility for finding you accommodation, but it need not be in the area where you applied (see pp. 43–5).

ISOLATION

The location of a permanent home is important and you should impress upon the council the necessity of having access to shops, schools and other people. When an authority promises to move you to another part of the borough, you may find yourself very isolated, particularly in rural areas. Try to make them offer you something suitable for a single parent, ask for somewhere with access to schools, nurseries, shops, relatives, etc.

STANDARD OF HOUSING

As we said above, you will usually get only one offer if you are housed by the homeless persons' unit and this will usually be from the worst housing stock. Standards vary a lot from area to area, and even within one district you may be offered a flat in need of complete redecoration or a newly painted house. The local authority would rarely admit that a property was uninhabitable or allow you to refuse the offer on those grounds. However, you are within your rights to refuse an offer of accommodation if it is 'prejudicial to health' – if you can prove that it will affect your health or the health of your dependants. In order to prove this, you will have to get support from an environmental health officer – and they are employed by the council – or you may be able to get an independent surveyor or environmental health officer to help you, if you can find one. If you or any of your children are in bad health, you could get a doctor to support your refusal on medical grounds. In addition, you can lobby individual councillors by going to see them or writing to them, and they may be able to persuade the homelessness unit to make another offer. As a last resort, you may call in the Press, but after a long struggle to get a tenancy of your own, it may seem easier to accept what is offered. It may be easier to make a deal with the council to accept the offer if they do some repairs before you move in. If you agree to their doing the repairs after you have moved in, you could wait months. Some local authorities will make grants to help with decorating, which means you could save money by doing the work yourself, and in some cases you can get grants from the DHSS. Ask the homelessness officer about the possibility of getting these grants and how you apply. Alternatively, you may get a decorating allowance in the form of rent-free weeks. If you decide you want to refuse the offer, do not hand back the keys straight away. The homelessness officer will usually discuss with you the reasons for refusing and you can assess whether it is worth fighting. You must be prepared for the possibility of being declared intentionally homeless if you refuse an offer of accommodation.

SIZE

The size of the property you will be offered is dictated by how many dependants you have, what sex they are, and their ages. As a rule, two children of different sexes would not be expected to share a room. If you are pregnant, it is possible, but not certain, that the council would take into account the fact that there will be another child. Alternatively, you may be expected to apply for a bigger place when the child is born, but a transfer for reasons of overcrowding could take years, as the rules about size only apply when the council is offering a tenancy and do not mean that you will get an immediate transfer.

WHEN YOU ARE ACCEPTED BY THE COUNCIL FOR REHOUSING

When the council accepts you as homeless, they should interview you in order to find out where you want to live and what sort of property you would like. They should also find out whether you have any special requirements, for example, a ground-floor flat for health reasons. Unless you have special needs, the answers that you give to questions about gardens etc. will probably not affect what you get. You may still have to wait in a refuge or in temporary accommodation for some time before being offered a tenancy. The length of time depends on where you are going to live and the amount of housing stock available. It is worth hassling the homelessness unit every so often to ask them when you will get your offer, as they may respond to pressure. They will eventually give you the address of a property and ask you to go and see it, after which you will be expected to sign the tenancy agreement. It has happened that women have been asked to sign for the tenancy before actually seeing it: don't – this is probably not lawful and if you are threatened with being declared intentionally homeless, get legal advice. You may be asked to pay a week's rent in advance, but if you are on supplementary benefit, do not worry about having to find the money, as you can claim it in full.

TRANSFERS

If you already have a local authority tenancy, you can still apply under the Housing (Homeless Persons) Act when you leave home, but you may prefer to apply for a transfer to another property.

The advantage is that it will probably be of a higher standard than accommodation offered to homeless people, and if it is your own tenancy the local authority will be more sympathetic to this course of action. It is also a way for women who are being harassed or attacked by men they do not live with to get away and move to a new place. There are different types of transfers, most of which depend upon getting the agreement of the local authority. All local authorities will accept applications for transfers, but the likelihood of getting one depends on which local authority you are dealing with. Some do not have procedures for emergency transfers and expect you to wait years for another tenancy. You should try to persuade them to deal with your case as quickly as possible if you cannot get them to agree to an emergency transfer, but remember that your argument is weakened if you ask to be moved close to home.

The disadvantages are, firstly, that it is possible to get a transfer only if the tenancy is in your sole name; secondly, that they can take a very long time to arrange; and thirdly, that there are often complications with rent arrears.

Local authorities are very reluctant to offer transfers to women who have rent arrears. If it is your own tenancy, then you are solely responsible for the rent arrears even if your husband or boyfriend had agreed to pay the rent. This is a particular problem if you are not working, because while you are cohabiting you cannot claim housing benefit and therefore have no means of paying the rent. Your husband or boyfriend can claim the rent money, but you are responsible for the arrears – if you leave home because of violence you may run up rent arrears while you are away unless you can get benefit for two rents. You may be able to negotiate with the council to let you pay the arrears over a period of time at a certain amount each week. If they are not sympathetic, try to get someone from Women's Aid or social services to put pressure on them to give you a transfer despite the arrears. Some authorities will freeze your responsibility for the rent while you wait for a transfer, but this is not the norm.

MANAGEMENT TRANSFERS

These are dealt with by the district housing office and are generally quicker than applying through the ordinary waiting-list. Go to your district office, explain the problems you are having and tell them you are in urgent need of a transfer. Before the district office takes any action, they may ask you to provide some evidence of violence in the form of medical reports, police reports, or a court order which you obtained because of the violence. If you cannot provide these, then try to get them to accept statements from witnesses or a solicitor's letter instead. If you are in a refuge, or have a social worker, you can get them to put pressure on your district office. Once they have agreed to a transfer, keep in regular contact to check on what is happening and how long you will have to wait.

On some estates the estate manager can organize a transfer locally but only within the same estate. If you can find two estate managers who are both willing, they may be able to organize a swap from one estate to the other, within the same borough. Where there is no procedure for emergency transfers, this is probably the quickest way to get one.

TRANSFER WAITING-LIST

The waiting-list for transfers is for people who have a council tenancy and want to move. If you want to transfer to another council property, you can go on to the waiting-list by applying at the local housing department. Everyone on the list is given points according to their need and this affects how long they have to wait. It could be up to ten years in some areas. Although some women are advised by the council to go on the transfer waiting-list, it is not a solution in an emergency.

PRIVATE SWAPS

Most local authorities have a list of tenants who want to swap their home for another one. If you look at the list you will find the name, address, type of property, size, whether it has a garden, etc., and you can contact the tenant yourself. Some people advertise in shop windows or local newspapers, particularly if they want to move out of the area. This sort of transfer is arranged by the tenants, but the council has to approve. It can be done through the district housing officer. The disadvantage is that another woman is possibly left in a vulnerable position, and you must be sure she will not tell anyone where you moved.

RECIPROCAL ARRANGEMENTS

Within London there is a scheme called the Inter-Borough Nomination Scheme which means that an authority can refer you to another borough in London, as long as it subscribes to the scheme, and then it will have to accept a tenant from that area in the future. There is a system of reciprocal arrangements in the rest of the country, but the disadvantage is that you have to rely on the council itself to arrange it and they are very wary of accepting more tenants than they refer.

MOBILITY SCHEME

This is quite a recent scheme which allows local authority, new town and housing association tenants to move to other areas of the country. To get on to the scheme you must already be a tenant of one of these authorities and you must have to move for reasons of employment or for 'social reasons'. It is possible to apply when you do not actually have a tenancy but do have a commitment from the council to offer a tenancy, so there is a transfer of responsibility from one local authority to another. It is up to the local authorities involved to decide whether to accept your application on these terms. In order to apply nationally (it operates on a county level also), you can get an application form from the council and check on their list what areas are in the scheme and where you want to move. Housing association tenants should ask at the association office for a form, if it is part of the scheme. The drawbacks are, firstly, that it is entirely voluntary and discretionary on the part of the authority involved; each has to decide whether to become part of the scheme and both authorities can reject an application, although they have to give their reasons. Secondly, the receiving authority may not be able to offer any accommodation immediately and an applicant may have to wait for months. A few authorities have said they will consider domestic violence sufficient 'social grounds' for entry into the scheme, so it is worth finding out from your council whether this is so.

GETTING THE TENANCY INTO YOUR NAME

You can transfer to another tenancy only when your existing one is in your sole name. The tenancy can be put into your name either in the divorce court, if you are married, or by consent. This applies whether it is a joint tenancy or the man's. Since the 1980 Housing Act, the local authority cannot legally take any action to transfer the tenancy from one partner to the other, so you have to wait for it to be decided in the divorce court, if you are married. If you are not married, there is no procedure for getting the tenancy into your name. In practice, local authorities are attempting to resolve this problem in different ways: some insist, if you are married, that you wait for the divorce court to settle the question of the tenancy; some will rehouse you elsewhere and leave the man with the old tenancy; some will evict both of you and rehouse whoever has the children elsewhere; and some will insist that you get an ouster injunction to remove the man and return home. You should always refuse to do this, as an injunction does not alter the man's rights to the tenancy, and if you are not married there is no way that you can end his right to the tenancy and keep your own rights to it. In practice, some authorities threaten him with eviction, which often serves to persuade him to give up his half of the tenancy, or they just take the tenancy away from him. However, if the man were to challenge his eviction in court, he would probably win. This problem applies to married woman and to cohabitees who have a joint tenancy and, as yet, no permanent legal solution has been found.

ENDING A JOINT TENANCY

A court decision in 1982 established the legal precedent that one joint tenant can give up a joint tenancy without the consent of the other, or even their knowledge. This could be used for you to make a 'deal' with the local authority to give up the tenancy so that your partner would no longer have any right to be there and then the authority could rehouse you elsewhere. The disadvantage could be that your husband or boyfriend could give up the tenancy for you both. You would then be unable to get a transfer and you would be in danger of being declared intentionally homeless.

REMOVING THE MAN FROM YOUR TENANCY

Before you get a transfer to another tenancy the council will usually expect you to have an unoccupied property to hand back to them. In some areas the council will come to evict your boyfriend or husband if he has no right to remain in the property but, generally, you will be expected to take this action yourself. There are two ways in which it is possible for you to remove the man, but both involve court proceedings.

Firstly, using domestic violence legislation, any woman can get an ouster injunction to remove the man if he has been violent. Once he is out of the house, the council will be more sympathetic towards offering you a transfer. You should only be able to get a transfer if the tenancy is in your sole name but, as mentioned above, some local authorities will transfer you if you are a joint tenant, although this is not strictly lawful. Secondly, cohabitees with their own tenancy can evict the man from the home as he has no tenancy rights at all. Married women would not be able to do this as a husband has an automatic right to live in his wife's tenancy. Both these options may take some time and you may have to find somewhere else to stay – with friends, in temporary accommodation or in a refuge – while a transfer is sorted out.

THE WAITING-LIST

Everyone has a right to apply to join the waiting-list for council housing. If you already have a council tenancy, you would more likely apply for a transfer, but if you have no tenancy of your own to transfer, or do not live in council property, you can join the waiting-list. When you apply, your housing need will be assessed and you will usually be given points to show how near the top of the list you are. It could take years to get an offer of accommodation this way, so it is not a very hopeful option for women leaving home because of violence. Some authorities will house only women from the ordinary waiting-list, which means that they are not accepting you as homeless under the Housing (Homeless Persons) Act. For example, in Luton and in Chelmsford, the council may tell you to return home after getting a court order to remove the man. If you cannot get a court order, they will expect you to join the waiting-list. In some areas where there is a large housing stock, this would mean a wait of only a few months, during which time you could wait in a refuge or with friends. In other areas it could mean an average wait of up to three years or more. If you are told to apply to join the waiting-list and you are therefore not being classed as homeless, you must get the decision in writing as to why they are not accepting you as homeless. Then you will probably need advice as to what action you can take if those reasons indicate that the council has not fulfilled its statutory duty.

HOUSING ASSOCIATIONS

Housing associations are organizations which use public money to provide housing but are independent of the local authority and do not have any duties under the Housing (Homeless Persons) Act. They may be large or small and usually operate in a specific area. They are quite common in large towns and cities but are few and far between in rural areas. Housing associations make their own policy about whom they will accept as tenants: some cater exclusively for single people, or for couples, or for people with children. They can accept women who are from outside the area and who have been refused by the council, and they are, therefore, a very necessary alternative for women escaping from violence. Some refuges rely heavily upon housing associations rather than arguing with the council.

The following are ways in which you can apply to a housing association.

REFERRAL BY THE COUNCIL

The council usually has some nomination rights to at least one housing association in the area. This means that if they have accepted responsibility for rehousing you, they can refer you to one. Housing association property is often in better condition than local authority property, so you may specifically want to get a housing association tenancy. In this case you should ask the homelessness officer to refer you.

SELF-REFERRAL

You may be able to approach the housing association yourself and apply for a tenancy. This is much more difficult, as they have only a limited amount of property and a large number of prospective tenants. Some close their waiting-lists for part of the year and some do not even have a waiting-list. Some accept only council nominations. However, it is worth contacting them and giving them your details, as it is timing that is important and you may be lucky.

REFERRAL FROM OTHER AGENCIES

Some housing associations will not take self-referrals but will take them from 'recognized bodies'. It is up to the housing association to decide which these are and it is worth finding out and contacting one of them. Women's Aid is sometimes regarded as a recognized body.

SHORT-LIFE PROPERTY

Most housing associations have some short-life property which is let temporarily. It is property which is owned by the housing association and left empty until they start work on converting it, and may be in very poor condition. An association will not often offer a short-life property to an individual, but a sympathetic one may respond to an emergency. It is more likely that they would pass on short-life property to agencies, like Women's Aid, or to local short-life housing co-ops, or keep it empty.

TRANSFERS IN HOUSING ASSOCIATION PROPERTY

If you are already a housing association tenant it may be possible, if the housing association is a large one and covers a large area, for the association to transfer you to another tenancy of theirs. If you think this may be possible, then go to the housing association office and discuss it with them. Again, before you can transfer to another tenancy you will have to have the tenancy in your name only, unless the housing association has a special policy for dealing with relationship breakdown. The same problems apply for married women and cohabitees who have joint tenancies in housing association property as in council property regarding the transfer of the tenancy to the woman's name, but it is worth asking to find out whether the housing association is sympathetic and can help.

HOUSING CO-OPS

Short-life co-ops were set up to use short-life property owned either by the council or by housing associations. They usually operate in one specific area and are most common in large towns. You can find out if one exists in your area by asking at the housing department or a housing association office. To refer yourself, you would normally just have to go to one of the meetings. If you are worried about going, you should contact someone from the co-op and introduce yourself first. There is usually a secretary whose name is advertised. Like housing associations, each short-life co-op is run differently and caters for different groups: some do not accept children; some do but will expect women to share with other families. For example, there is a short-life housing group in Bristol which accepts women from the refuge, and two women who already know each other may apply to share the same house. The property is usually in need of some repairs and decoration, but in some co-ops this work is carried out and paid for by the co-op. The money you pay in rent, which is usually nominal, goes into a fund to do this work. Because the property is only short-life it is obviously only a temporary solution, but in the larger co-ops you can almost guarantee to be rehoused in another property when the licence runs out on the one you are occupying. If you are lucky, you may get a very long licence of up to five years, but this is not the norm and it is more likely that you will have to move about every six months. This can be very unsettling for you and the children. However, if you have not got any children, it can be a long-term solution and you will probably be housed with other single people.

Long-life housing co-ops provide permanent and decent housing to tenants, who run the co-op themselves. Each tenant is expected to take part in the running of the co-op, which may mean attending weekly or monthly meetings. The advantage is that the tenant controls her own housing.

Long-life co-ops are less common than short-life ones because they are harder to set up, but you should ask the housing aid centre whether there is one in your area. The council may refer you to a co-op themselves or you can refer yourself and join by attending one of their meetings. The process of getting a tenancy may be a very long one, as the tenant is expected to be involved in the conversion and decoration of the property. Depending on your assessed housing need, it could be years before you finally move into a flat or house. Going to a housing co-op is therefore a long-term solution unless you find one that has property it wants to get rid of quickly. It is worth finding out.

PRIVATE RENTED ACCOMMODATION

The availability of private rented accommodation depends on which part of the country you are looking in. It is particularly difficult to find in London and other major cities, and also in small rural areas. Women without children will usually find it easier, as many private landlords do not allow children. The private rented sector can mean anything from a rented house to a room in a hotel, and many single women are forced into living in hostels because there is no alternative.

SECURITY

If you are looking for a permanent home, you will probably want a secure tenancy, but many landlords in the private sector have found ways in which to avoid granting security of tenure. When you consider moving in somewhere, ask whether you will have a rent book, and whether there is a written tenancy agreement which you can study. Does the landlord have access to your room? Do you have a resident landlord? Is it a fixed-term tenancy? All these things affect whether you will be secure or not. There are many different types of tenancy which mean different things, so check what sort it is before you take it on, and be clear about what the agreement with your landlord is. If you need advice, you can take the agreement to an advice agency in the area or to the housing aid centre at the local authority.

FINDING RENTED PROPERTY

Flats, houses, rooms and bed-sits are advertised in local papers and shop windows. Alternatively, you may go to an accommodation agency, which will have lists of property on their books. Be wary of these agencies taking money from you: they will ask for a commission for finding the flat, which could be as much as a hundred pounds. They will sometimes ask you to pay them a sum of money before they will give you an address. It is up to you to decide whether to pay this, but you may not get it back.

RENT

In private property the rent is usually much higher than in council or housing association property. Before you move in, you will usually be asked for a deposit (if the property is furnished, you may be able to get this from social security), and for a month's rent in advance, which you may be able to get from the local authority. Once you have the tenancy, you can apply to have the rent registered if you feel you are paying too much and you are a secure tenant. Find out from the council housing department how to do this, or go to an advice centre, CAB or local tenants' association – they may be able to help you with your case. Your rent will be registered at a fair rent level and may go up or down as a result. Your landlord cannot evict you because you have reduced the rent as long as you are a secure tenant, and it is illegal for him to charge more than the registered rent. Nor can he evict you for rent arrears if you do not pay the higher charge. Before registering the rent, you should find out what the average rents in your area are to check that you are not paying less than average, and find out from the housing department whether the rent is already registered. You should not register the rent if you are not a secure tenant, as your landlord could evict you if the rent was reduced.

CLAIMING YOUR RENT

Some landlords will not accept tenants who will be claiming their rent from the local authority, and will accept only tenants who are working. This means that they are on the fiddle in some way, and unless you can hide the fact that you are claiming, you will lose the place. In order to claim the rent, you will need some sort of evidence that you are paying it, and your landlord may be reluctant to give it, but you should always ask for a rent book or at least a receipt.

HOLIDAY AND TEMPORARY LETS

In order to avoid the responsibility involved in creating secure tenancies, landlords will often offer only holiday or temporary lets, which means that you have no security and have to leave after the term of the licence. You should take these only in emergencies, as you cannot expect the tenancy to be extended. If you are going to approach the council for help, they may consider that you have made yourself homeless intentionally by accepting a tenancy which you knew was only temporary, and they will look at the reasons why you moved in originally to establish the cause of your homelessness.

SHARING

Magazines, newsletters and shop windows will often advertise rooms in shared houses. This is usually for women without children, but sometimes a woman who has children herself will want another woman to share her home. You can find where to look for these adverts through Women's Aid, Gingerbread or other one-parent organizations. This can work well if both parties are willing to share, but you should sort out all the arrangements before you move in, to avoid arguments later. Single people taking rooms in large houses will be either joining a household that operates communally, moving into a family home, or living independently with other single people also living independently. What you choose depends on what you want.

HOME OWNERSHIP

In order to buy a house, you may sell your old home and intend to buy another one with your share of the proceeds, or may want to take out a mortgage on a new home, or take over the mortgage from your husband on your old home. If you have enough money, you may be able to buy outright, which is quite straightforward if you have a solicitor, but can take months. If you do not have enough money to buy outright, you will need to get a mortgage from a bank or building society. Many of these institutions may still be prejudiced against women and it is very difficult to get a mortgage without a large, secure income.

TRANSFERRING THE HOME TO YOUR NAME

When you separate from your husband or boyfriend and get the house put into your name, you become responsible for all the mortgage repayments, unless you are getting maintenance. You should visit the building society to discuss arrangements to pay off the debt. If you are not working, and are claiming supplementary benefit, you can claim the interest on the mortgage from the DHSS and you will then have to discuss with the building society whether they are willing to accept interest-only payments. The Abbey National building society has a policy of accepting interest-only payments for as long as necessary following relationship breakdown; other building socieites may not be so sympathetic.

TAKING ON A NEW MORTGAGE

If you do not work and are claiming benefit, you will find it almost impossible to take on a new mortgage unless you can persuade a building society or bank to lend you the money to buy a house on the basis that you have a large lump sum to pay as a deposit. Alternatively you may be able to get a joint mortgage with another woman if you are both working and have a reasonably high combined income.

SQUATTING

Squatting involves moving into an empty house with no authority from the owner or landlord. There are a great many empty properties all over the country, but there are not many that are open for people to move into.

Breaking into an empty house is illegal, so if you are going to squat, do not break in. Many women squat through desperation if they cannot find any other accommodation. Squats are rent-free, you can claim social security using the address of the house you have moved to, and there are some groups in large towns who are willing to give practical help and advice to people who want to squat in empty property. There are many disadvantages to this method of finding accommodation, the first being that you can never know how long you will be able to stay. Some landlords will evict squatters immediately, but others may leave you there until they want to sell or convert the property. The same applies to local authorities and their attitudes towards squatters in their property. If you have a lot of possessions and furniture, you may find yourself having to move it around all the time. You are also in danger of being declared intentionally homeless if you apply as homeless to a local authority at a later date, because they will often say that if you left your home to go and live in a squat, you made yourself homeless intentionally.

Squatting is not a good idea for women with children, as it can be very unsettling to have to move from one place to another. But some women find they have no alternative. If you are in this position contact one of the squatters' organizations for advice on what your position is legally, and you may also get some practical help from them.

4. MONEY

The most urgent problem when you leave home, apart from finding somewhere else to stay, is money. If at all possible, take some money with you, or borrow some, to keep you going for the first few days. If you have had to leave with little or no money, you can get help from social services or social security at any time of the day or night. The type of help and who provides it will depend on whether you normally have your own income, whether you have an address and whether it is at night or during the day.

EMERGENCY PAYMENTS DURING THE NIGHT

If you leave at night and you have no money, you can ring the emergency *social services* in your area. If you do not know the number or if there is none, then you can go to the police, who will put you in touch with them. A social worker should be able to find you somewhere to stay temporarily and can also give you an emergency cash payment. It is designed as a payment to keep children out of care, but in practice it is given to women with children when they have no other resources. Women without children cannot usually get such payments.

In areas where there is an emergency *social security* team, the social worker will contact it to give you some money. You may be able to contact the emergency social security team yourself if you are staying in a refuge or with friends, but you will have to get the number from the police or social services. Someone from the emergency social security team will come and visit you, and if they consider that there is an urgent need they will make a cash payment to last until you make a claim.

The procedure for making emergency payments at night varies considerably in different areas: if you do not know what it is, the general rule should be to get in touch with social services.

EMERGENCY PAYMENTS DURING THE WEEKEND

In most areas the same procedure applies at weekends as at night, as the social security office is shut. However, in London you can get emergency payments on Saturdays from 9 a.m. to 10 p.m., Sundays from 2 p.m. to 10 p.m., and from 6 p.m. to 10 p.m. on weekdays from the office at Marshalsea Road, London SE1 (Telephone number: 407–2315).

EMERGENCY PAYMENTS DURING THE DAY

If you leave during the day you should go to the local social security office to claim what is called an urgent-needs payment. It is better if you can give them the address of where you are staying, so you would normally go to social security after you have approached the council, gone to friends or found a refuge. If you are intending to claim benefit, the urgent-needs payment should be sufficient to last until your appointment with the benefit officer. In order to get an urgent-needs payment, you will probably have to wait a very long time in the social security office, but do not be put off asking.

MOVING AWAY

You may decide to leave home and move a long way away, either to friends or to a refuge in another area, in which case you will need money for travel. This can be provided by social security, social services or housing departments, if they arrange accommodation in the form of a travel warrant. Out of office hours it is very hard to arrange a travel warrant, although social services have been known to give them. If they refuse, you should ask them to provide accommodation, if you have none, until the next day. Within office hours, you can go to the local social security office, ask for a travel warrant and tell them why you want to go. They should give you a Giro cheque to the value of the tickets, including any bus fares etc., or they may give you a voucher for the train fare. Social security have a duty to provide travel warrants if it is necessary for you to leave, but you have to have an address to go to, so organize where you are going before approaching them. This can be done if you are in touch with a refuge, as they will contact social security to say that they are expecting you. Occasionally, social security officers insist that they have proof in writing of where you are going, but you can probably get round this, particularly if the refuge or your friends contact them by phone.

WEEKLY INCOME

Your weekly income will consist of money from paid employment, private income, maintenance from an ex-partner, some kind of benefit, or a combination of these. Most women when they leave home or are left in the matrimonial home will claim some sort of benefit, unless they are in full-time paid employment. Even if you are working, you may be eligible for housing benefit – which is like the old system of rent and rate rebates – and/or family income supplement (FIS) if you are on a low income.

CLAIMING BENEFITS

Most benefits are paid only if you have an address, and you will probably need some kind of identification, such as a marriage licence or child-benefit book. In cases of domestic violence, the benefit office can get copies of marriage or birth certificates. You may not have to prove your identity to the benefit office, but you may have to when cashing your money at the post office.

Which benefit you claim will depend on whether you have children, whether you have an income, how much that is, and whether you are living with a man. You are entitled to claim insurance benefits like unemployment benefit while cohabiting, but you are prohibited from claiming supplementary benefit if you are living with a man as 'husband and wife'. This is called the cohabitation rule and is explained more fully later (pp. 76–7).

Unless you are on quite a high income, you will probably claim some sort of benefit. It may cover all or part of your income and all or part of your housing costs. It may meet weekly needs or be a one-off payment; some are means-tested and others are not. This chapter deals with the different sorts of benefit, and also deals with other sources of income which may be full-time or part-time work, or maintenance – a payment made by an ex-husband for a wife and/or children.

UNEMPLOYMENT BENEFIT

You can claim this if you have been working and have given up or lost your job, and you remain available for full-time work, and you have paid enough stamps in the relevant year. It will be granted only if you have paid the stamp for a single woman, not if you have been paying the married woman's stamp. It is paid for up to 312 days of unemployment, and is not income-related, but a fixed amount for everyone. You cannot get unemployment benefit for six weeks after leaving your job unless you have a good reason for leaving. If you have left home because of violence, you should explain that this is why you had to leave your job, and the 'six-week rule' should not apply. If it is used against you, you can claim supplementary benefit in that time, but it will be at a reduced rate. If you go back to work in the same tax year, your unemployment benefit will be taxed. Most women who have children do not bother to claim unemployment benefit, as you have to claim supplementary benefit to make up your income anyway, and the only difference is that you have to make two claims. Women who are cohabiting will claim it, because you can get it while you are living with a man.

HOW TO CLAIM

In order to claim, you should go to the unemployment office, and they will either interview you immediately, make an appointment for you or, if you have no children, they will give you a form to fill in and send back. This form is extremely long and you may need advice to fill it in; it asks for all the information they want about your last job and your living circumstances. If you have an interview, you should take with you proof of where you live, your national insurance (NI) number and your wage slips for the last few weeks or months. They will ask you about your last job, but they are not allowed to ask personal questions. Afterwards, they will give you a signing-on card and tell you when each week to sign on.

WHO CAN CLAIM

In order to claim unemployment benefit, you must show that you are available for full-time work and can accept a job if a suitable one is offered to you. This means registering at the unemployment office. If you do not have dependent children you will have to register for work even if you are not eligible for unemployment benefit, unless you are disabled or are within ten years of retiring and have little prospect of getting a job, or are exempt for any other reason. Women without children will automatically get unemployment benefit if they are eligible, although they may get supplementary benefit too.

If you have children, you will be asked whether you have made adequate child-care arrangements for the time you would be at work – this is before you even get a job! If you say no, they will ask more detailed questions and you may lose your benefit if they do not think you have made sufficient arrangements. You will be expected to register for work and you can register at the job centre, but this is voluntary and many people do not bother. Even if you are not eligible for unemployment benefit, you should register at the unemployment office as being available for work (if you are), as you will then get your insurance stamp paid, which pays for your pension.

You may decide to keep your job but to take some time off, as holiday or compassionate leave, if your employer agrees, or you may need to take some time off sick.

SICKNESS BENEFIT

Since April 1983 you get statutory sick pay (SSP) from your employer for the first eight weeks in any tax year, after which you get sickness benefit which you have to claim from the DHSS. If you are ill for a second period after you have received SSP, you can claim it again, but you will get it only for a total period of eight weeks in one tax year.

STATUTORY SICK PAY

If you are sick for four or more consecutive days your employer will be responsible for paying SSP. If you are unable to work because of sickness, you should notify your employer as soon as possible, first by telephone, then by letter. When reporting that you are sick, give the date on which sickness commenced, even if this was not a normal working-day. No SSP is payable for the first three days on which you would ordinarily have worked. If you are sick for four or more days your employer must decide if SSP is payable to you. For example, no SSP is payable to an employee who is over the minimum state pension age or who has average weekly earnings of less than the lower weekly earnings limit for NI contributions liability. There are other reasons why the employer may withhold SSP. If your employer decides not to pay SSP, he will tell you, so that, if appropriate, you can apply to the DHSS for state sickness benefit instead. If SSP is payable, the amount due will be calculated by reference to one of the three weekly rates of SSP depending on your average weekly earnings, and the number of days of sickness after the three waiting days. PAYE and NI will be deducted from SSP in the same way as for ordinary earnings. You will be required to complete a self-certification form for a period of sickness lasting four to five days. For a longer period of sickness, a doctor's certificate will be required from the eighth day and at weekly interviews.

STATE SICKNESS BENEFIT

If you are not eligible for SSP you will claim state sickness benefit by filling out the form SSP1(T) which you can get from your doctor or the DHSS. State sickness benefit is a flat-rate payment which you will get if you have paid sufficient stamps in the relevant tax year, paying the single woman's stamp. You should not need a sick note for the first week as you can sign the form yourself, but after that you should get a doctor's note.

If you are relying on sick pay or unemployment benefit as sole income, it is very unlikely to cover your needs as defined by supplementary benefit scale rates. Similarly, if you are on a very low income, from whatever source, and this is lower than the supplementary benefit scale rate, you become eligible to claim supplementary benefit. Payment of housing costs (rent and rates) should be dealt with separately, and only women with incomes below the scale rate, not including rent and rates, are eligible for supplementary benefit.

SUPPLEMENTARY BENEFIT

SB is a welfare benefit designed to bring the income of everybody not in full-time work up to a minimum level. If you are on unemployment benefit or sickness benefit or have a low income or no income at all, you may be eligible. It is strictly means-tested and you are paid the difference between the amount of income you have and this minimum level. There are various additional requirements benefits for things like diet, heating, laundry, for which you may also be eligible. If you are on SB wholly or partly, you automatically become eligible for free school meals and various health and welfare benefits. These are also available to women on low incomes. The system is very complicated and it needs specialist knowledge to know exactly what you are entitled to; there are dozens of extras which could be added to your weekly income. The DHSS officers should tell you what you are entitled to, but often they do not. You can get advice as to what you may be entitled to from CABs, advice agencies or the local authority welfare rights officers.

WHO CAN CLAIM

You can claim SB for yourself and your children unless
a) you are under sixteen;
b) you are in full-time work of more than thirty hours a week;
c) you are living with a man as 'husband and wife';
d) you have a large sum of money saved – this is called your 'capital resources' and the amount you are allowed to keep changes every year (in November 1983 it was £3,000). If you have had a lump-sum payment in a divorce settlement, you may find that you can no longer claim until the capital is reduced. Normally, the DHSS will not allow you to claim for a period equivalent to how long it would take to spend your capital at the rate of supplementary benefit each week, unless you spend it on necessary capital goods. The sort of goods you are allowed to spend capital on and still claim SB will be household things, not 'luxuries' like holidays. You should get advice on how to spend any capital you have before actually spending it, as you may lose entitlement to benefit.

In order to claim SB you must register for work and sign on at the unemployment office as being available for work unless
a) you are over sixty years of age;
b) you are a single parent;
c) you are sick or disabled.

If you are signing on, they will pay you fornightly; if not, you will get paid weekly by Giro at first and then get an order book which you can cash for as long as your circumstances do not change. There are now also facilities for your benefit to be paid straight into your bank account.

MAKING A CLAIM

Whether you are claiming from a refuge, from temporary accommodation or from a friend's house, the process of claiming will be the same. There are three different ways of claiming:

1. Go to the local DHSS office and ask at reception for an interview to claim SB. You may be seen the same day but this can mean a very long wait. Most officers will make you an appointment. If you are absolutely penniless, you can ask for a payment to last until the appointment; this usually means a long wait too.
2. Ring up the DHSS and make the appointment yourself.
3. Get a form from the DHSS or the post office, fill it in and send it back. This means that someone will have to visit you before you get any money, which contributes to a delay of possibly more than a week, so it is not a good idea if you are short of money.

THE FIRST INTERVIEW

If you have children, you will usually be interviewed by the liable relatives officer; if you do not have children you will be interviewed by someone who works on the section. You should take your child benefit book, if you have one, wages slips for the last few weeks, if you have been working, proof of where you are living, and proof of any savings.

When you are interviewed by the LRO, if possible take a friend with you (or an advice worker) for moral support. You should be able to insist that you are accompanied into the interviewing room. It is the job of the LRO to establish whether or not there is a man who is liable to support you and/or the children. You will be asked to give a description of the man involved so that they can contact him in order to get him to pay maintenance. You should stress that in no circumstances should they tell him where you are staying. You cannot be forced to ask him for maintenance, but the DHSS can make the man pay them maintenance for you and the children while they are paying you benefit. If you are not married they will be concerned only with the maintenance for the children. You may be subjected to personal and offensive questioning but you do not have to answer personal questions. You do not have to give details about your husband or boyfriend; try to be evasive but co-operative – you do not have to say where he works or lives. If you are uncooperative, the DHSS cannot refuse benefit, but they may make life difficult by asking you to go to the office every week to hang around for payment.

HOW YOUR CLAIM IS WORKED OUT

The amount you get depends on your needs and the needs of your children, and how much money you are already getting from other sources. The benefit will be the difference between the two, so that your income is brought up to the basic minimum level.

Needs are assessed according the DHSS scale rates which change every year and are supposed to cover normal requirements (food, clothes, entertainment, fares, everyday expenses). There is a householder rate, which includes an amount for heating, lighting, cooking and hot water, for women who are responsible for paying rent, and a non-householder rate for women living in other people's homes. There are different rates for children of different ages, and you should claim for dependent children under sixteen, while children over sixteen should claim for themselves unless they are in full-time education.

LONG-TERM RATE

After one year of claiming, you will become entitled to the long-term rate of supplementary benefit which is slightly higher, provided you are not required to sign on for work. This will apply only to women who have children or do not have to sign on for some other reason. You can have a break of up to eight weeks and still be able to claim the long-term rate: for example, you may work for six weeks in the year and stop claiming SB for that time, but when you go back to claiming, you will be on the long-term rate. If you have a break for more than eight weeks, then you will have to claim for a further twelve months before getting the long-term rate. If your husband was claiming and did not have to sign on for work, you can use that time to qualify for the long-term rate after you have separated, but you must claim within eight weeks of being on your own.

ADDITIONAL REQUIREMENTS

There are also weekly benefits for what are called additional requirements that you should be asked about when you first claim at the DHSS. The officer is not likely to ask you, so it is just as well to know what these additions are before you go, so that you can say you want to claim them. Each is for a specific need and is for a specific amount of money: for example, all people over eighty years old get an extra 25 pence per week! Others are for heating, if your home is particularly difficult or expensive to heat, laundry, diet, if you or your children need a special diet because of illness, baths, blindness, HP payments, home help, storage of furniture, etc. If you do not claim any of these because you did not know about them, you can get them paid up to a year in arrears. When you go on the long-term rate these additions are reduced by 50 pence a week.

So your needs are assessed as normal requirements for you and your children plus additional requirements.

INCOME AND EARNINGS DISREGARD

Your income includes all the money that you and your children are receiving from any source, for instance, child benefit, pensions, unemployment or other benefit, maintenance payments, and income from part-time work.

When your benefit is worked out, you are slightly better off if you have another source of income, as you are allowed to keep some of it, while the rest is taken off your benefit. If you have sub-tenants, lodgers, or boarders, then there are set rates of how much will deducted from housing benefit but not from SB. From other earnings there is a set sum which is deducted and this changes at various times:

1. The first £4 of income from part-time earnings are disregarded, and if you are single parent, half your weekly earnings between £4 and £20 will also be disregarded; so the maximum you can earn is £12, plus expenses connected with work which are also disregarded: for instance, child care, fares to work, and meals.
2. Child benefit, one-parent benefit and maintenance are all fully deducted, as are other benefits.
3. The first £4 of a pension is disregarded.

SINGLE PAYMENTS

Single payments are lump-sum payments from SB to enable you to pay for things which are not covered by weekly SB payments. They are available to anyone who is on SB or who would be entitled to it if they claimed it. Granting single payments is entirely discretionary, so it is up to the benefit officer who deals with your application to decide whether you really need a single payment, and if so, how much you should get. As a result, it is difficult to compare different amounts given to different people. When you move into a new home, you may get much more or less than another woman moving the same week.

There are several points to remember when you claim for a single payment:

1. A benefit officer may have to visit you in your home before you receive a single payment and it can take weeks before you are visited.
2. If you have no children or have been working recently, you will probably be refused a single payment, unless you can prove your circumstances to be really exceptional, like moving to a new home.
3. It is generally best to claim one single payment for all the things you need. Many SB officers will turn down a request for a single payment if you have had one in the last six months, even if the last one was very small.
4. You will not normally be given a single payment if you have sufficient savings over £300 to pay for the goods. If you do not have enough you can get a payment for the difference.
5. They have to tell you in writing of their decision.
6. You can appeal.

WHAT CAN BE CLAIMED

Anything that is an exceptional need and likely to arise only occasionally can be claimed. There are certain categories for which payment will not be made, which include school expenses, costs of a motor vehicle, rental or installation of a telephone, TV or radio rental or licence costs, holidays, repairs to a council tenancy, or medical requirements. You must show that you need the item, do not already have one or something similar and you have not unreasonably disposed of one that you did have. Here are examples of expenses that can be covered by special payments:

1. Heating appliances.
2. Redecoration.
3. Furniture.
4. Floor coverings (this means lino).
5. Fuel debts – but this is very rare.
6. Electricity reconnection charges.
7. Rent arrears – but again this is rare.
8. Removal expenses, if you provide three estimates.
9. Travel expenses on certain journeys to visit relatives in hospital or prison. You can also get money to move to another part of the country provided you have an address to go to.
10. Funeral expenses.
11. Costs of starting work, fares to interviews, work clothes, etc.
12. Clothes and equipment for a new baby.
13. Storage of furniture. If you have to leave home and do not intend to go back you can put your furniture in storage. You will have to get three estimates of the cost of storage and it can be paid for up to a year by DHSS.
14. Clothes for yourself and the children. It is now much more difficult to get single payments for clothing as they are theoretically included in your normal requirements. However, single payments for clothes are still available if your clothes have been lost or destroyed or if you have had to leave home in a hurry and have left your clothes behind. Some officers insist that before they will give a single payment for clothes when you have left home because of violence, you will have to prove that you have been back home with the police for protection, and salvaged what you can. If your clothes have been destroyed or sold, they should then give you a payment. You can argue that you cannot go back to get your things because of serious risk of violence and you may win an appeal if your application is refused.

When you apply you should write a list of all the things you are asking for, with prices from a reputable shop, details of your circumstances and of what payments you have had in the past. The payment will either be a Giro cheque made out to you, or, if you have provided estimates, it could be made out to the shop. However, there is no check that you spend the money on what you applied for.

MOVING TO A NEW HOME

If you get rehoused in a new home and you left your old home with nothing, then as long as you are claiming SB, you can ask for a single payment to provide the necessities for moving. When you know the date of your move write a letter to the DHSS office where you are claiming, telling them that you are about to move and what you are claiming for. Include as much as you can think of in the letter. You should get beds and bedding for each of the family, a chair each and a dining table, cutlery, crockery, cooking utensils, towels, kettle, iron, fire and fire guard (if there is no central heating), saucepans, wastepaper bin, cleaning utensils, etc., etc. – put everything you can think of that can be considered necessities. You will normally have to provide estimates for a second-hand cooker and new beds, though the money you get will very rarely cover the full cost of these items. You should also apply for the connection charge and delivery charges. If you have proved that you do not have any of these items, you should get a payment, but how much seems to depend on luck more than anything else; everyone gets a different amount. They will give you a breakdown of what they are giving you with the amounts allocated, but some women get much more than others, just as some women have to fight for it and other women just have to ask. If you are unhappy about the decision or the amount you can appeal.

If you already have the necessities in storage, you can apply for the money to pay for their removal, but you will not get money to buy new things.

Once you have moved you can then apply for the so-called luxuries like wardrobes, floor coverings, curtains, armchairs, etc. This will involve a visit from the benefit officer, so you should make a claim to your new local DHSS office as early as possible, to avoid delay.

There are a great many single payments which you may be eligible for; if you are not sure about them ask at the DHSS office or contact an advice agency.

APPEALS

You are bound to come across problems when claiming SB. The first is when you think your claim has been worked out wrongly. You should receive, with your first payment, a form saying how it has been worked out, but if you are still not sure how it is done, then you can ask for a detailed breakdown. If you think that it is wrong, you can appeal to a tribunal. You can get help with this and any other problems with the DHSS from local advice agencies. At the same time you can, if it is an obvious mistake, ring or go to the office and explain the mistake; ask them to correct it and then withdraw the appeal. You can also ask for a *review* of the decision, which it is better to do in writing. This can be done at any time, and if the decision is changed, you can get arrears of benefit up to a year. If the decision is not reversed, you can take the case to appeal, as long as you do this within twenty-eight days.

WHAT YOU CAN APPEAL ABOUT

Mistakes in your weekly benefit are often caused by mistakes on the part of the SB officer, which are corrected as soon as you appeal and do not go to a tribunal.

Single payments cause the most common type of appeal, because the amount of single payment depends on the discretion of the officer. It is important to make clear to the tribunal why you asked for a single payment and what it was for. You should then explain why you think the decision taken was unjust. Take evidence of your savings and general financial position to show that you cannot afford to buy the items you have requested a single payment for. If you have never had a single payment before or have not had one for a long time, you should tell the tribunal this.

Cohabitation can provide two grounds for appeal: either you are not cohabiting, or you are cohabiting but there are exceptional circumstances (for example, the man you are living with refuses to support your children in which case you might get some money for them, but not for yourself).

APPEALS TO A TRIBUNAL

If you want to take an appeal to a tribunal, you must do it within twenty-eight days of the DHSS's decision being made. You must write to the benefit officer and include as much information as possible in the letter because it will be one of the documents that the members of the tribunal consider. Also include in your letter your request that the appeal be heard quickly.

You can appeal against any decision made by the SB office. To do this, you should write a 'letter of appeal' and send it to your local SB office. The letter should be headed 'Notice of Appeal', and addressed to the Clerk of the Supplementary Benefits Tribunal at your local SB office. Then you should explain:

a) What the decision was that you wish to appeal against;

b) What you think is wrong with the decision, why you want it to be changed and what you want the new decision to be;

c) Any relevant information – particularly financial information such as what you get already from SB.

The SB office can reply to your letter in one of two ways. Firstly, they may tell you that they have reconsidered their decision and decided in your favour, in which case they should send an explanation of the new decision, and tell you whether or not your appeal has been withdrawn. If you disagree with the new decision, you should write another letter of appeal. Alternatively, you may get a date for a hearing by the appeal tribunal. The hearing will usually be within four weeks, but if your appeal is urgent – as are cohabitation appeals, for instance – you should ring the SB office frequently and press for an early date. If the date you are given is inconvenient, you can write and ask to have it altered. Together with the date, you will get all the papers to do with the case, so you can study what the SB officer is going to say. If you receive no reply to your appeal, you should ring the SB office and insist that the appeal is dealt with quickly.

THE TRIBUNAL

The tribunal has three members who are supposed to be independent of the DHSS. You should always be heard by three people, unless you agree to two. One is chosen by the local trade unions, another is chosen by the government for her/his local knowledge (for example, a businessman or a vicar) and the third is the chairperson. You do not have to attend the hearing – it can be held in your absence – but in practice it is very important that you do go, or that someone else goes in your place. You can take one or two people with you as friends, advisers, or representatives; all three of you are allowed to speak, and most claimants stand more chance of success with their appeal if they take someone along with them. You can get advice and help with your appeal from Women's Aid, advice centres, etc. You can also call witnesses, and you, your advisers and witnesses can claim travelling expenses and loss of earnings.

The tribunal is held in private. The SB office case is put by a presenting officer, and you can ask questions, then put your own case. It is usually best to speak for yourself and use your advisers to help you out. You cannot get legal aid to apply for representation at the tribunal, but you can get legal advice: this is the 'green form scheme'. The decision of the tribunal should be sent with an explanation within a week. The decision is binding; this means that you cannot appeal on the same facts again, but if your circumstances change, you can ask for the decision to be reviewed. If you think the tribunal has made an error in the law, you can appeal within three months to the Social Security Commissioners – but you must get legal advice before you do this.

FRAUD

Prosecution for fraud can sometimes feel as if it is being used as a threat by an SB office, if they think you have been deliberately lying to them. Do not let this put you off appealing, if you think they have made a wrong decision. If the SB office does decide to try to prosecute you for fraud, you should find yourself a sympathetic solicitor and apply for legal aid. If you are acquitted, you should apply to have your SB restored.

COHABITING

The common problems, for single parents, of cohabitation discriminate openly against women. Although it is not likely to be a problem when you first leave home, it very often crops up later. A woman living with a man as husband and wife has no right to claim SB for herself or her children, even if the man does not give you any money. It is sometimes difficult to define whether you are living as husband and wife, but there are some points which the SB department use to help them decide.

1. Do you live at the same address? If you do, then do you share domestic arrangements? If you are a lodger, sub-tenant or housekeeper then you are not cohabiting.
2. Is the relationship stable? The DHSS tends to assume that a relationship of over two or three weeks is stable, but you could argue this point.
3. Is there financial support? The DHSS may consider shared expenses to be financial support.
4. Is there a sexual relationship? The officer should not question you about your sex life, but if you are not having a sexual relationship with

the man you should say so; you would not usually be considered to be cohabiting if this is the case.

5. If you are looking after a child you have had by the man you are living with this is strong evidence that you are cohabiting, but does not in itself prove it.

6. If the neighbours think of you as married and you encourage this, it is evidence that you are cohabiting.

IF YOU ARE SUSPECTED OF COHABITING

You will be visited by a benefit officer, who will question you and the man. The officer may use what you say at a tribunal, so be careful of what you say. If he thinks you are cohabiting, your benefit will be stopped and there is a possibility that you will be asked to repay what you have had. If the decision is wrong, you can appeal and you should. The benefit officers often carry out very intimidating and humiliating investigations, which may force you into not appealing, but it is always worth doing it, if you are not living with a man.

RENT AND RATES

Money for rent and rates is no longer covered by SB unless you are a home owner, long-lease holder, co-owner or boarder in a hostel. Non-householders are assumed not to be paying rent but receive a nominal rent addition from supplementary benefit.

Boarders are people classed by the DHSS as living in hostels, hotels or similar establishments. This means that if you are living in a bed-and-breakfast hotel or in a refuge, you may be classed as a boarder and get the boarder rate of SB rather than the householder rate. If you are not clear about your status, the social security will tell you when you make your first claim. The amount you get will depend on what area you live in, how the benefit officer interprets your claim and what type of hostel you are in. You should ask the benefit officer to explain to you how it is worked out, and if you think it is wrong go to a CAB, advice agency or the welfare rights officer in the council. Some hostels will have an arrangement for the rent to be paid direct from the DHSS to the hostel. They will tell you if this is the case and the money you get will be adjusted. If you are working and you go to a hostel, you can still claim rent and rate rebates from the council for the rent and rate portion of the hostel charge.

CLAIMING IN TEMPORARY ACCOMMODATION

You can claim for rent and rates in temporary accommodation in the same way as you would in permanent accommodation. However, when you leave home, you might find yourself responsible for both the rent on your temporary home and for part, or all, of the rent on the place you have left. In these circumstances it is possible to claim for rent on two tenancies. When you make your claim for housing benefit or boarders' allowance, you should ask about this.

If you are given bed-and-breakfast accommodation by the council, you will usually be classified as a boarder by the DHSS, and if you are claiming, you will get all your money from them. Arrangements for paying the hostel charge vary according to the policy of the local council. Usually they will pay all or part of the rent. If you are offered bed-and-breakfast accommodation by the council, always ask if you are expected to make any contribution towards the costs, and how to pay this.

RENT AND RATES FOR HOUSEHOLDERS

If you are classified by the DHSS as a householder, they will tell you to apply to the local authority for payment of your housing costs, which are your rent and rates but do not include charges for lighting, heating, hot water or cooking. If you are expected to pay for any of these services with your rent, you will have to pay them from your SB. The money you get for your rent and rates is called housing benefit. When you claim SB, you will be told how to apply for housing benefit. Otherwise you can go to your local authority and apply directly to them for housing benefit. If you have no income or an income which is below the SB scale rates, the DHSS will issue a 'certificate' to authorize payment of housing benefit, which they send to the council. Private and housing association tenants will get a payment equal to the full rent and rates, and council tenants will go on to rent direct, as the council pays the rent to itself. If you have an income which is more than the SB scale rates, you will not be eligible for supplementary benefit and your housing benefit will be worked out as for standard rent and rate rebate cases. In cases where this means you will lose money, you may be eligible for housing benefit supplement. This is designed to bring your income up to the level of SB, so you should not lose money by being on housing benefit. It is calculated by the DHSS, so it is better to approach them first, rather than the local authority. Also, payment can be backdated to when you first approached the DHSS, but not if you went to the council first. Once you are eligible for housing benefit supplement, you automatically become eligible for additional SB payments: single payments, health and welfare benefits, etc.

Even with an income which is above the SB scale rates and sufficient to cover your housing costs, you may be eligible for housing benefit in the form of rent allowances and rate rebates. To do this you must apply to the local authority.

Payment

The local authority should process your claim within fourteen days, but this is unlikely to happen. If you are eligible for housing benefit for all the rent and rates, you should ask for an interim payment, so you can pay your rent in the meantime. You will normally get paid monthly, but you may be able to get your payments fortnightly or weekly if you request it.

ILLEGAL TENANCIES

When you apply for housing benefit, whether or not you are 'certificated', the local authority will check their records to see if you are the registered tenant. This will mean that if you have an 'illegal' council tenancy (for instance, you are living in the flat of a friend who has moved on), then the council will not pay housing benefit to you. They will pay it only to the lawful tenant.

LODGERS AND SUB-TENANTS

If you decide to take in lodgers or sub-let part of your home and you are claiming benefit, then the amount you charge will usually affect the level of benefit you get. A lodger is defined as someone who is part of your household or who pays a substantial amount for meals as well as paying rent. A sub-tenant is defined as inhabiting a separate household. When you claim family income supplement (FIS), the profits you make will be treated as income, but allowance is made for your expenses. If you are claiming SB and/or housing benefit, the deductions made will depend on whether you have a lodger or a sub-tenant.

A lodger will be treated as a non-dependant, which means that the money you receive will not affect SB but a fixed amount will be deducted from your housing benefit.

Any rent you receive from a sub-tenant will be deducted from your rent before your rent allowance is calculated. Rent does not include rates, water rates, payment for meals, heating, lighting and cooking. Standard deductions are made from the rent you charge the tenant before it is offset against the rent you pay, depending on which of these services you provide or pay for. This is to allow for expenses involved in providing services. The amount you get in rates from the sub-tenant is offset against the rates you pay before your rate rebate is worked out. So when you have a sub-tenant, the amount you get is deducted (apart from the allowance for services) from your housing benefit. If the amount you get is greater than your entitlement to housing benefit, then the excess is treated as income by the SB office.

BENEFITS AVAILABLE ONLY TO WOMEN WITH CHILDREN

Child benefit is paid to all parents and consists of an allowance for each child. It is usually paid monthly, but it can be weekly if you request it by filling in the form on the back of your book. It can be paid to you or your husband, or it may be in both names. When you leave home, it is best to take your child benefit book with you as it can be used as identification and it is a certain income. If it is in your husband's name, you can get this changed. If you leave it behind and you have the children with you, social security can cancel the benefit and transfer it to you. This is not means-tested and there are no qualifications for getting it – no matter how much you earn, you can still claim child benefit. If you are on SB, however, it is deducted from your benefit.

Single parents are entitled to *one-parent benefit* which is an addition paid on top of child benefit. To get this you have to be separated for thirteen weeks, and then the social security will accept you as self-supporting. It is well worth applying for this when you have left home or been left alone. If you are on SB it is deducted from your weekly allowance.

If your children are at school, some costs can be reclaimed by *school benefits* if you are on SB, FIS or a low income. These are the costs of school meals, school uniforms, journeys to school if they are over three miles, and one school trip per year, but they are all discretionary and whether you succeed in getting any of them depends to some extent on where you live. To apply for them you should go to the local education office where the forms will be available. For children over sixteen who are at school or in further education you may get an *educational maintenance allowance*, which is also discretionary, but most children should get this. For other benefits for children including children under school age, see pp. 81–3.

DISABILITY BENEFITS

There are some benefits that are available to you if you are disabled or if you have a child or other dependant who is disabled. To find out more about such benefits, you should ask at the social security office, or a local advice agency or contact the Disability Alliance (see Appendix I for addresses).

Among the benefits you can claim which are not means-tested and for which you don't have to have made any contributions are:

1. *Attendance Allowance*. This is paid to you if you need frequent attention or supervision. In order to qualify, you must have been disabled for six months. The allowance can be paid for a child aged two years and over, provided that the child needs substantially more care than a child of the same age who is not handicapped. The attendance allowance for a child is paid to the person with whom she lives, normally the mother.
2. *Mobility Allowance*. This is paid to you if you cannot walk or find it extremely difficult to walk because of physical handicap.
3. *Invalid Care Allowance*. This is paid if you are of working age and remain at home to care for a severely disabled relative who is receiving an attendance allowance. You will get an amount for yourself and extra for dependants. You will not get this if you are living with a man.

HEALTH AND WELFARE BENEFITS

All these benefits are explained fully in forms available from the DHSS, or from some doctors' surgeries, post offices, advice centres, CABs, etc. Each benefit is available to different categories of people. The health benefits are not discretionary, but the school ones are. They are available to those on SB, FIS or with low incomes, but each benefit form defines low income as something different.

1. Free prescriptions are available for women over sixty years, children under sixteen, expectant mothers, mothers with a child under one year, people receiving SB or FIS and their dependants, and people on very low incomes. To get these you have to fill in the prescription form or get an exemption certificate.

2. Free dental and optical prescriptions are available for women over sixty years, children under sixteen, expectant mothers, mothers with a child under one year, people receiving SB or FIS and their dependants, and those on low incomes. People under twenty-one, expectant mothers, and mothers with a child under one year can get free dental treatment: tell the dentist you want to claim and send the form to social security. For glasses, get a form from the optician. This will mean you can get one of a limited choice of frames.
3. Fares to school are payable to those who have children attending a school more than three miles away from home.
4. Free milk and vitamins should be given to expectant mothers and children under five in families receiving SB or FIS or on a very low income, and to families with more than two children under five. Disabled children, and children in nurseries or with child-minders may be able to get some free milk. You get seven pints of milk per week or two packs of dried milk.
5. Free school meals are available for those on SB or FIS or on a low income.
6. Fares are refunded if you have to visit a close relative or child in hospital; this benefit is available to those on SB or FIS. If you keep the tickets and go to the hospital social worker, she should refund the money.
7. School-clothing grants are available in some areas to families on SB, FIS or low income.
There is much more detailed information than this available from the DHSS on the forms they provide, which are available from DHSS offices, post offices, some doctors, clinics and libraries.

OTHER BENEFITS

There are many other benefits which you may be able to claim from the DHSS; this list may be helpful:
1. *Maternity grant.* A single grant of £25 payable when you have a baby.
2. *Maternity allowance.* Payable for eighteen weeks around the birth of a baby, if you have paid enough NI contributions.
3. *Invalidity benefit.* Payable if you are still unfit to work after six months on sickness benefit.
4. *Non-contributory invalidity pension.* Payable if you have been unfit to work for six months but have not paid enough NI contributions to get sickness benefit.
5. *Housewives' non-contributory invalidity pension.* As above, for a woman

living with a man, except that you have to prove that as well as being unfit to work you cannot perform your normal household duties.
6. *Widows' allowances.* Payable for six months to all widows whose husbands had paid enough NI contributions. Continued after six months for those who have dependent children or are over forty. You cannot get these allowances if you are living with a man.
7. *Child's special allowance.* Payable if you are divorced and your ex-husband, who was paying maintenance for your children, dies. This allowance depends on whether your ex-husband has paid enough NI contributions. You cannot get this allowance if you are living with a man.
8. *Guardian's allowance.* Payable if you are looking after an orphan. No contributions are necessary.
9. *Retirement pension.* Payable if you are over sixty, provided you have paid enough NI contributions. In some circumstances, your husband's NI contributions can count towards your retirement pension.
10. *Death grant.* Payable when someone dies, provided that the dead person or her/his spouse has paid enough NI contributions. If the dead person is a child, her/his parents' NI contributions are taken into account.

FAMILY INCOME SUPPLEMENT

If you are working more than thirty hours a week you are not entitled to claim supplementary benefit, but you may, nonetheless, have a very low income and in this case you may be eligible for FIS ('fizz'). This is a social security benefit paid to parents in full-time work who have children living with them. 'Full-time' means at least twenty-four hours a week for single parents, and thirty hours a week for others.

You will be eligible for FIS if your gross weekly income is less than a certain amount, called the prescribed amount. It is means-tested, so the amount you get depends on how much income you receive. Your gross income for FIS purposes includes:
a) earnings;
b) child benefit and one-parent benefit;
c) any income the children have (other than maintenance);
d) attendance/mobility allowance;
e) rent rebates/allowances;
f) the first £4 of a war disablement pension.
So, income for FIS is not the same as income for SB. The FIS you receive will be half the difference between the prescribed amount and your gross income.

IRREGULAR INCOME

If your earnings vary a lot from week to week, you can make an assessment based on a longer period, so that you can work out an appropriate average income. If you work part of the year (for instance, as a teacher), you should be able to claim for the full year as long as you make your claim in the term time, or at a time when you are working.

MAINTENANCE PAYMENTS

These are normally averaged out over the previous six months, but if they are irregular you can ask that FIS be paid to you for an initial period of four weeks, taking into account the maintenance you get over that period. After that time, you can apply again, when you have a better idea of what the maintenance will be. If it is not clear and will not be clear, you can ask that you continue applying on a four-weekly basis for as long as necessary.

HOW TO CLAIM

To claim FIS you should ask for the form for FIS at the DHSS office, advice centre or post office, and it will say on the form what the 'prescribed' income level is for you. You send this form to the address on it and enclose your pay slips for the last five weeks, or two months if you are paid monthly. If you are self-employed send your latest tax assessment and trading accounts. If you have just started a new job, then evidence of two weeks' earnings should be enough. When your benefit has been worked out you will get an order book to cash at a local post office. Payments run for fifty-two weeks regardless of circumstances. There are maximum payments, so you should ask what these are. If you are working at least twenty-four hours a week, it is worth claiming FIS, as in general you will be financially better off. It is worth trying to increase your hours to twenty-four to bring you within the limit. You should claim as soon as you become eligible. FIS cannot be backdated. Even if the amount of FIS you get is very small, it is still worth claiming, as a successful claim entitles you to various health and welfare benefits.

APPEALS

If you feel you have been wrongly refused or given too little FIS, then you can appeal. You must write within twenty-eight days to your local social security office saying that you want to appeal against the decision (give the date of the decision) regarding your application for FIS. Put 'Notice of FIS Appeal' at the top of the letter. If you put 'urgent' at the top of the letter, in red ink, it will usually be dealt with more quickly.

MAINTENANCE

Many women do not want to have any contact with their ex-husband or boyfriend and certainly do not want to claim any maintenance. You do not have to; do not let anyone – DHSS, solicitors, etc. – pressurize you into making a claim if you don't want to.

IF YOU ARE MARRIED

Your husband has a duty to maintain you and any children of the marriage. The maintenance can be paid on a voluntary basis by the man or be endorsed by a court order. If he is not giving you any money or you are afraid that he will stop giving you money, you can apply to the court for a maintenance order. We explain how to do this on pp. 127–31. The man is legally bound to pay if a court order is granted, though it does not necessarily mean you will get the money – he may choose not to obey the order. Maintenance payments can be arranged in different ways:

1. They can be deducted from your husband's wages by the court and paid to you by the court. This is usually done only if he is a persistent bad payer.
2. The man can pay the maintenance regularly into the court and you have to collect it.
3. He can send it directly to you.
4. As your maintenance is deducted from your SB, your husband can pay it straight to the DHSS. If he is unreliable, it is safer for him to pay the DHSS direct, as it is their responsibility to take him to court for failure to pay.

If you are on SB, the DHSS may ask you to apply for a maintenance order. You do not have to do this if you do not want to. The DHSS can take your husband to court to get him to pay maintenance direct to them, which is nothing to do with you: it is a private matter between the DHSS and your husband.

IF YOU ARE NOT MARRIED

You can apply for an affiliation order to get the father of your children to pay towards their maintenance. Maintenance paid for the children may be paid either to you or to the children. Either way, the money is deducted from SB and FIS, but for tax purposes it is to your advantage to have the order worded 'to the children' (see p. 87).

HOME OWNERS

If your ex-partner is paying the mortgage on the home you are living in, any capital repayments he makes to pay off the mortgage will be regarded as maintenance by the DHSS if you claim benefit. Therefore, this will be regarded as part of your income. If he pays the capital direct to the building society, the benefit officer can ignore that income.

TAXATION

As this is a very complicated subject, you may need to get expert advice from your employer, CABs, unions or the local tax office. The amount of tax you pay is calculated on the income you receive from April of one year to the following April. A portion of this is not taxed and this amount is called your tax allowance. Your tax allowance is specified in your tax code which is shown on your tax assessment and pay slip. You can check the code, which is three figures and then a letter, which means different things. Your tax allowance is the first three figures of your tax code, multiplied by ten. After the allowance has been taken off your income, the remainder is divided by 52 (if paid weekly), or 12 (if paid monthly), and you pay a bit of tax each week or month; this is called Pay As You Earn (PAYE).

If you are a single parent, you are entitled to two allowances: the single person's allowance and the additional personal allowance, which together add up to the same as the married man's personal allowance, so let your employer know if you become a single parent. If you are cohabiting, either one of you can apply for the additional allowance.

There are other allowances to which you may be entitled which increase your total tax allowance:

a) housekeeper allowance (usually given only to men);
b) dependent relative allowance;
c) age allowance;

d) blind person's allowance;
e) son or daughter's services allowance.

If you earn less than your tax allowance, you should not pay any tax at all. This also applies if you are a student.

Each year there are changes in the tax allowances and sometimes in the rate of taxation, so it is important to check that you are not paying too much tax. In order to make sure, you need to fill in a tax return. You get these from your local tax office – your employer will tell you where this is. If you write to them, explain your circumstances. This is particularly important if your situation has changed, for instance if you have left home.

MAINTENANCE PAYMENTS

Maintenance payments paid voluntarily are not taxable, but if there is a court order or signed agreement, the man can claim tax relief on the payments, and you will have to pay tax on what you receive. If the payments are over a certain amount, then the Inland Revenue can allow the man to deduct the tax before he pays the maintenance and you can get a tax rebate if you don't pay tax already yourself.

If the payments are made to you for the children, you may have to pay tax on them as they become part of your income, but if the maintenance order is made to the children, it is their income and they will not pay tax on it unless it exceeds the single person's allowance.

SAVINGS

If you have savings, try to get the best rate of interest on them. Building societies generally pay reasonable interest, but tax is deducted from the interest at the standard rate by the building society. This saves you trouble if you are paying tax already, but if you aren't paying income tax (for instance, if you are on SB or a student grant), it's probably better to put your savings somewhere where tax is not deducted from the interest, such as in a bank deposit account or a post office.

5. LEGAL PROTECTION

If your partner is violent or aggressive towards you or your children, there are several types of legal action that you can take in order to try to stop him attacking you. When you are deciding which is the most appropriate course of action to take, you should first consider what you want to do. Do you want to stay at home with or without him? Do you want to leave the home and return when he has been ordered to leave it? Would it be best for you to try to get a new place to live where he cannot find you? Will it be necessary to have legally binding arrangements for the children and will you want to claim property from the matrimonial home? You may want to seek legal protection by getting a court order which requires him to behave in a particular way, and you may want to end the marriage as well. When you first think of taking legal action against your partner you will not necessarily know what you want to do in the long term about your marriage or relationship, and you should not feel obliged to make any major decisions too quickly. However, before starting court proceedings, it is important to consider what you hope to achieve by going to court, bearing in mind the limitations that your circumstances put on the types of legal action available to you. Factors that affect your choice are, for example, the severity of the violence and whether it was physical or mental, whether you shared a home with the man, whether you are married to him and whether it is likely that legal action will be effective in protecting you from any further assaults.

It is important that you understand what you can achieve using the various legal proceedings. Solicitors may make suggestions that are not necessarily in your best interests, or which may not be effective, so use your own judgement when deciding to go to court. Bear in mind that there are other options open to you apart from seeking legal protection through matrimonial court orders, such as applying to the local authority for rehousing. However, you should not delay going to court if you want to, because it can be much more difficult to win your case even a few days after the incident that led to your decision to take legal action. Immediate and sympathetic legal advice, therefore, is essential when you are thinking of using the law to help you. We describe the various types of legal action that you may take and the ways in which you can get free or cheap legal help.

WHAT KIND OF LEGAL ACTION SHOULD YOU TAKE?

If your main concern is to get legal protection from violence, you might think that the police would be the best people to turn to. However, when you call them because you have been assaulted by the man you live with, they may not want to get involved. Although they could arrest and prosecute him for a criminal offence, if you are not seriously injured they may just warn him not to misbehave and they might suggest that you go to the Magistrates' court and prosecute him yourself or take proceedings for an injunction. Even if he is taken to court by the police, he may not be dealt with very severely. He will probably be fined or 'bound over to keep the peace', if he has not been to court before. This does not amount to much protection for you, unless the court appearance itself is enough to deter him from further assaults.

As an alternative you can use matrimonial or civil law to apply for an injunction, which is a court order that tells him either to take a particular action or to stop doing something. It is possible to take your case to court even if you have no witnesses who saw what happened, but if you have any injuries, you should see your doctor, so that she can report on them to the court later on. In addition to court orders giving protection, you can ask the court to make decisions and orders about such questions as who should have the children, live in the home and have the property in it. This can be done immediately, without waiting for divorce or separation proceedings to be finished. In an urgent case, it is possible to get a court order made within one day, without your partner being present, although you will then have to go to court again soon afterwards when he has been informed about the proceedings. You can apply whether you are married to, or just living with, the man whom you take to court. If you are neither married to him nor living with him as man and wife, you can still apply for legal protection but your choice of legal action is more limited.

For protection, you can get orders stipulating that he does not assault, molest or otherwise interfere with you or the children; that he leaves the matrimonial home; or that he keeps a certain distance from your home, for example, outside a half-mile radius.

To clarify the position regarding the children, you can be granted interim custody of them until the full custody hearing; he can be ordered to return them to your care and control; and he can be ordered not to remove them from your care and control.

For rights in relation to the home, he can be ordered to allow you into the home you shared, not to part with possession of the home or its contents, nor to damage it or its contents (this can be done only through divorce or judicial separation proceedings).

To provide for the cost of living, he can be made responsible for all the outgoings of the matrimonial home (if you are married), and an interim maintenance order can be made that he pays an amount of money each week for the children and maybe for you.

Another type of proceeding that you can use is an application to have the children made wards of court. This is useful if you are afraid that they may be snatched from you, particularly if you think they may be taken out of England and Wales. You can also get an injunction forbidding him to assault you and a maintenance order for the children as part of these proceedings – as long as you no longer live together.

PROTECTION

You can use the Domestic Violence and Matrimonial Proceedings Act 1976 in the County court to get a non-molestation injunction which orders your partner not to assault or molest you or the children. You can apply for an exclusion (or ouster) injunction that orders him to leave the home and to stay away. If necessary, the court can order him to let you back into the home, either to get your possessions or to stay there. He is only ordered to leave temporarily, usually for three months, during which time you should sort out the legal position regarding his rights to the home, if he has any. If you are married, your husband has a legal right to live in the home even if it is in your name.

An exclusion order can be renewed for another limited period if that is appropriate. If you are not married, your partner must have been living with you until recently as though you were husband and wife. Sometimes the judge is not asked to make the court order because your partner or his lawyer suggest that he gives an undertaking to the court instead. This is a promise that he will do the things that you are asking for court orders about. Although the court will treat a broken undertaking in the same way as a broken injunction, and can imprison him for it, the police may not treat it as seriously. It is difficult, however, to persuade the judge not to accept an undertaking on the first occasion that you go to court, unless your partner has broken court orders or undertakings before.

Only married women can use the Domestic Proceedings and Magistrates' Courts Act 1978 to get similar orders from the Magistrates' court. A personal protection order tells your husband not to assault or threaten to assault you and/or the children. An exclusion order tells him to leave your home and not to return. The magistrate can order him to let you back into the home using this procedure and you can also ask the court to make an order for financial provisions, by making a separate application which can be heard at the same time. When you apply for maintenance, the court must consider whether custody and access orders should be made. It is not possible to get orders on these questions under the Domestic Violence Act. However, the Domestic Proceedings and Magistrates' Courts Act is more limited in the protection it can give than the Domestic Violence Act, because the conditions under which you can use it are very specific. Where you have been threatened but there has not been any physical violence, it may be easier to use the Domestic Violence Act. We go into the merits of the County court or the Magistrates' court legislation later on in this chapter.

If you definitely want to end the marriage, you can apply as part of divorce or judicial separation proceedings for a non-molestation injunction and 'ouster' injunction which orders him to leave and stay away from the home. You can also sort out questions of custody, access and property. If you have religious or other objections to divorce, you can apply for the same orders when you apply for a decree of judicial separation, which does not end the marriage but leads to long-term decisions about the children, the home and property. If you have not been married long enough to get a divorce, you can still get a judicial separation. If you and your husband are buying a house or have bought one, you are probably entitled to a share of what it is worth. The divorce or judicial separation proceedings will establish your share of the matrimonial property if you and your husband disagree about it. In order to protect your right to your share of the home and prevent him from selling it, you can register an interest in it at the Land Registry if it is not in your name. This is complicated, so it is best to get advice from a solicitor.

If you are neither married to, nor living with, the man who has assaulted or bothered you, it is not possible to use the matrimonial laws or Domestic Violence Act to seek protection, unless you have only recently been divorced, in which case you may be able to return to the divorce court. You can apply under the Guardianship of Minors Acts for a non-molestation injunction and custody if he is the children's father or if he is assaulting them. Otherwise, you must take out a summons for assault and claim damages in the County court, applying for an injunction as part of these proceedings. The procedure is similar to that for getting an injunction under the Domestic Violence Act, but it is more complicated and you cannot get the power of arrest attached to the order, which, as we will explain later, may make it less effective. If you want to take action against aggressive neighbours, father, son or other people in your home, this is the appropriate legislation to use.

You do not have to take any legal action when you separate from your partner if you do not want to. You may just want to get rehoused and not bother with court orders. It is up to you to decide whether legal action would be useful as a deterrent in case he troubles you again, or whether it is necessary to get court orders about the children, your home or possessions. Any necessary arrangements can be sorted out between yourselves if you are able to discuss it with him, or you can just go away and set up a new home with the children without making any formal arrangement, if you do not think there will be any problems later on.

CHILDREN

If you are married, you and your husband have joint parental rights over the children. Either of you can apply for custody or access at any time, although the application will not necessarily be granted. If you think he might try to take the children from you, either by snatching them or by legal proceedings, it is advisable for you to establish a legal right to have them as soon as possible. You can get interim custody, which is a court order that you are to have the children until the full custody hearing, or you can have them made wards of court. When you want to sort out the questions of custody, access and maintenance, if you are married, you can apply under divorce or judicial separation proceedings or you can use the Guardianship of Minors Acts in the Magistrates' court, County court or High Court. The County court and the High Court have the power to grant injunctions when orders on custody and access are made, but this is not possible in the Magistrates' court. You may get a non-molestation injunction which covers yourself and the children and an order that he stays away from the home. Alternatively, you can use the Domestic Proceedings and Magistrates' Courts Act to apply for custody, or access and maintenance, as well as orders giving legal protection.

Unmarried women automatically have sole parental rights over the children, which means that you can decide whether their father can have access to them, unless he gets a court order giving him access. If you want to apply for maintenance and are not married, you can only apply for an affiliation order (in the Magistrates' court), which is a finding of paternity and an order for child maintenance and/or a lump sum of up to £500 (at the time of writing this book). You can apply only if the father has been maintaining the child within the past three years or if the child is less than three years old.

EVICTION

If you want to order someone out of the home who probably has no legal right to be there, such as a man who came to live with you in a place that is in your name only, you can get an eviction order by taking possession proceedings in the County court. However, this does not give you the legal protection from assault that an ouster injunction using the Domestic Violence Act may give, or that you can get from a claim for damages for trespass or assault. Before you can apply for a possession order, it is necessary to end his right to live in your home and it is advisable to seek legal advice about this.

DOES A COURT ORDER GIVE EFFECTIVE LEGAL PROTECTION?

When you consider starting court proceedings in order to get legal protection from a violent man, you must assess whether a court order will have the desired effect. Effective legal protection will be possible only if the man you take to court is deterred from assaulting you again by the court order, or if the police and courts will help you to enforce the court order if he breaks it. Your opinion on the likelihood of your partner obeying a court order is the most likely one to be correct. If he does break it, the only effective way to ensure that you will be safe is for him to be arrested and locked up. The type of injunction that you get will affect the extent of help that you can expect to get from the police.

THE POWER OF ARREST

The court can attach the power of arrest to a matrimonial injunction under the Domestic Violence Act, the Domestic Proceedings and Magistrates' Courts Act, and divorce or judicial separation law, if the man has actually injured you or your children in the past and is likely to do so again. Power of arrest cannot be attached to an undertaking and is unlikely to be given on an order made in his absence. This power enables the police to arrest without a warrant anyone suspected of breaking the order and to bring him to court within twenty-four hours. At that hearing, the court will decide what should be done to the man for disobeying the court order. However, arrest is discretionary, which means that it is up the police to decide whether to make an arrest or not. Experience of trying to enforce injunctions has shown that police practice varies greatly, and many police officers will merely tell a man off or escort him from the premises and let him go again after he has broken an injunction. If there is a power of arrest they are much more willing to arrest him. Police are rarely willing to search for a man who has broken an injunction – they will consider arresting him only if he is still there when they arrive. If your injunction does not have a power of arrest attached, the police will generally arrest the man only if he has obviously committed a criminal offence, such as assault. If the police do not make an arrest, it is your responsibility to enforce the court order by going back to court and applying for another hearing at which the court will decide what action to take against him for breaking the order.

COURT ATTITUDES

Although an application for an injunction should be heard as a matter of urgency, courts occasionally make you wait some time before it is heard, and even then you may not necessarily get the order that you apply for. Judges are generally willing to grant an order that you should not be attacked, but not to attach the power of arrest, even though this can make a lot of difference to the amount of help you can expect to get from the police, and, therefore, to the effectiveness of the order. Some judges believe that just a telling-off is enough to deter a violent man, or they are sympathetic to his attempt to blame the woman for the attack. If a man offers to give an undertaking to the court, this is often acceptable to the judge, even though you would prefer an injunction. The power of arrest cannot then be granted, and in fact tends to be given only when an order has been broken or when the violence has caused very serious injury. A survey of the way in which the Domestic Violence Act was put into practice during the first two years after it was passed also showed great regional variations in the way it was interpreted. For example, women were more likely to get the injunction they asked for and a power of arrest if they lived in London; and some judges would grant whatever order was requested, while others were reluctant to make anything more than a non-molestation order. Even if a man is arrested for breaking an injunction, it is up to the court to decide whether he should be punished for it. There was a decrease in the percentage of men arrested and imprisoned for breaking an injunction over the first couple of years after the Act was introduced. Courts tend just to give a warning when injunctions are broken, unless the man has been taken back to court several times already, and if he is imprisoned, it is unlikely to be for very long.

NON-MOLESTATION ORDERS

A non-molestation order, and the fact that you have actually taken your partner to court, will show him that you are serious and may deter him from further violence or aggression. It is worth getting one if you want to continue living with him or in a place which he knows about, or if he might go and harass you where you work. The police might help you if you have a non-molestation order, and you can always take him back to court and possibly have him sent to prison if there is further trouble. Councils often tell women to get an injunction either so that

they can return home or to prove that they are battered, but it is up to you to decide whether you want to get an injunction or not. When you see the solicitor, you can ask for a letter to be sent to the council stating your case, which the council might accept as proof that you are battered; and you can suggest to the housing officers that they get medical reports, social work reports or evidence from neighbours, rather than insisting that you get an injunction. Just your own evidence should be enough to get rehoused, but if you can produce any evidence like reports, witnesses or photographs, it may be easier for you. If the council insists that you get an injunction, there is no harm in getting a non-molestation order but courts are unwilling to grant exclusion orders if you do not intend to return home.

THE USE OF EXCLUSION ORDERS

A man can be excluded from the matrimonial home even though it is in his name and whether or not you are married. However, courts are not always willing to grant exclusion orders. They are unlikely to do so if you are unmarried, have no children, or if the home is in his name.

They may also refuse on the grounds that your case is not serious enough, or they may believe that you do not intend to return home. The case *Warwick* v. *Warwick*, heard in the Appeal court in 1981, made it clear that the Domestic Violence Act should not be used to get an exclusion order when actually you want to be rehoused, and do not intend to return home. A solicitor might advise you to get an exclusion order because she thinks your case is strong enough, but you should discuss whether it is advisable to do so if you know you do not intend to return home. The temporary nature of exclusion orders obtained under the Domestic Violence Act makes them difficult to use effectively as a means of getting a safe place to live on a long-term basis. If the man is the tenant, or if you are both tenants, an exclusion order does not end his right to the tenancy, even though he cannot live in the home for as long as the order lasts. He loses his right to the home only by being evicted for something like not paying the rent or for being noisy and a nuisance to neighbours, although it may be possible for someone to persuade him to give up his tenancy after an exclusion order has been made. If he owns the house or shares the ownership with you, he may be excluded for three months using the Domestic Violence Act, but only a divorce court can permanently end his right to live in the house. An ouster injunction made in the course of divorce proceedings can exclude him until the divorce is granted, when you may be given the right to live in the matrimonial home without him. If you alone own the house, he still has the right to live in it while you are married, but if you are not married then you may be able to obtain a court order evicting him from it.

Even if the man does not have the right to return at the end of an exclusion order, the problems that you might find in enforcing the injunction can mean that you are still not safe in the home. Experience has shown that very often the only way to be sure that a persistently aggressive man cannot continue to bother you is for you to move to an address where you cannot be found. This can be done by getting an order to make him leave and getting a transfer, if he does not have the rights to the tenancy, and if you are a local authority or housing association tenant. Otherwise, you should go to your local council and claim to be rehoused under the Housing (Homeless Persons) Act rather than going to court for an injunction. If they tell you to get an injunction and go home, but you are sure that you will not be safe where he can find you, you should tell them so. It may be necessary to get help from someone like a Woman's Aid worker, a sympathetic social worker or a solicitor in order to get the council to rehouse you. Ouster injunctions should not be used by local authorities to avoid their duty to rehouse you, but persistent argument may be necessary to enforce your right to rehousing.

CRIMINAL INJURIES COMPENSATION

The courts may order your partner to pay compensation to you in respect of injuries he has caused, although you are unlikely to get much if he is poor. You can also apply to the Criminal Injuries Compensation Board for compensation for any physical injury you have received as a result of violence within a family, whether you are married or not, provided that it was severe enough for you to be entitled to at least £500. However, it is only possible to get this payment if the person who was responsible for the injury has been prosecuted, in connection with the offence, unless you can show that there are practical, technical or other good reasons why a prosecution has not been brought. In practice, it is very hard to make a claim if he has not been prosecuted, and impossible if the incident was not reported to the police. In addition, you are unable to claim unless you had stopped living in the same household when the injuries were caused, and are unlikely to live with the man again. If you want to get advice and help in making a claim you can go to an advice agency, law centre or solicitor, to see whether they can help. Although full legal aid is not available for this, you may be able to get assistance from a lawyer under the green form legal aid scheme.

In order to make the claim you fill in the application form, which you can get from the Criminal Injuries Compensation Board, 10–12 Russell Square, London WC1B 5EN, and send it back to them. It helps if you can give details of any medical treatment that you have had or any witnesses to the attack. They will let you know how much compensation they think you are entitled to, or the reasons for refusing the claim. If you are not happy with this decision you should apply, within three months, for a hearing before the Board. You will have to make out your case to them, with the help of witnesses or other evidence if you wish to take any. You can go with a friend or legal adviser, but the Board will not pay for legal representation, although they may pay expenses to you and your witnesses. It is not possible to appeal against the decision made at the hearing.

GETTING LEGAL ADVICE AND REPRESENTATION

It is better to have a solicitor if you decide to go to court, although it is possible for you to do the legal work yourself if you want to. You may wish to conduct the case yourself if you cannot get legal aid. In a few cases, it is probably essential to have legal help – in disputes over custody or property, for example, or in wardship cases. Even if you do employ a solicitor, it is important that you understand what she is advising, and that you think the particular proceedings that are recommended will achieve what you want to do. Remember that you should be the one who tells your solicitor what you want, not the other way round. You may decide, after taking legal advice, not to take any legal action at all. Even if you are going to prepare your own case, it is a good idea to get legal advice first, so that you can be sure you are taking the proceedings which are the most suitable for you.

If you just want advice from a solicitor, you can often get this for little or no money, using the green form scheme. This enables you to have free advice if you are on supplementary benefit or a low income and you do not have too much capital, or to pay a small amount if you have a bit more money. Some solicitors do fixed-fee interviews, costing just a few pounds, which you must ask for at the start of the interview if you do not qualify for the green form scheme. Law centres and other advice centres often have sessions where you can get free advice from a lawyer even if you do have an income. These advice sessions will help you get the paperwork done for a court case, but give you limited rights to representation in court. You can, however, represent yourself in any type of court, if you want to. Some of the documents that you must use are standard forms available from court offices. For other papers that you need to write up yourself, you can find examples in legal books available in advice centres or libraries. There are specialist books which give details of how to take out particular types of court cases. Court officials can also give some advice about taking out a court case.

If you wish to employ a solicitor, she will tell you how much it is likely to cost to do the legal work, and whether you can get legal aid to pay the costs of the case. If you have no money, legal aid should be granted for most types of court case, except a simple undefended divorce. When you are working or have money invested, you may still be eligible for legal aid, but you might have to pay a contribution towards your legal costs. You will be called for an interview with the legal aid authorities about your means, which you must attend in order to get the legal aid to which you are entitled. When you are taking proceedings against your husband, his income and capital will not be taken into account, but you have to pay back the legal aid if you eventually get a lot of money from property settlement, unless your partner is ordered to pay the costs.

APPLYING FOR LEGAL AID

You fill in the forms, which you can get from the solicitor or the court, and send them to the court or to the Law Society who decide whether to give you legal aid and whether you must pay a contribution. In an emergency, it is possible to apply for legal aid on the telephone so that you can go to court on the same day. Legal aid for an emergency application is sometimes refused, however, which means you must wait for some time before going to court. When you go to see your solicitor, try to take the relevant documents with you – your marriage certificate, papers from previous court proceedings, rent book or tenancy agreement – and any evidence you may have, like medical reports or photographs of your injuries. It can be useful to have a photograph of your partner too.

FINDING A SOLICITOR

It is, unfortunately, still harder than it should be in some parts of the country to find sympathetic and competent solicitors. They need to be used to dealing with emergency situations affecting battered women, so it is useful to have one recommended to you. We hope that this book will enable you to know what to demand of your solicitor, who should be prepared to act quickly and to help you apply for legal aid which can be made available immediately. Your local Women's Aid group will have the names of good solicitors in your area. If you do not know how to contact your local Women's Aid group, WAFE will be able to help you. If you live in a city, you may be near a law centre which will be able to give you names of sympathetic and efficient solicitors, or may be able to help you with your case themselves. Your local CAB may be able to suggest a helpful solicitor from the Law Society's list of solicitors who do legal aid work. Social workers, probation officers, women's centres, libraries and other organizations sometimes keep lists of solicitors.

CHOOSING BETWEEN THE COURTS

Cases may be heard in one of three types of court – the Magistrates' court, the County court or the High Court. Magistrates are generally people chosen from the local establishment. They are not legally qualified except in big cities, but have a legally qualified clerk to advise them on the law. A 'domestic' case will be heard in private by two or three magistrates, who should include both a man and a woman. Magistrates can hear applications from married women for protection orders against a husband's violence, or for orders excluding him from the house. They can make orders on maintenance, custody, and access but they cannot hear divorce or judicial separation cases or make any decisions about ownership or tenancy of housing. County courts can hear applications from both married and unmarried women for injunctions against violence or harassment by men. They can also grant injunctions excluding a man from the house, or from a particular area. Most County courts can hear undefended petitions for divorce and judicial separation, and can decide the matters that go with these cases – custody, maintenance, access, and ownership or tenancy of housing. Your case will be heard by one judge, probably in private. The High Court hears defended divorces and judicial separation proceedings, and decides the matters that go with them. (However, very few cases end up in the High Court.) It also deals with applications to make children wards of court.

Once you are sure what legal steps you want to take, there are some areas in which you will have a choice about which court to use. It is worth asking your solicitor whether there is a choice of courts for your case. For example, if you are a married woman and want to get a court order protecting you from your husband, you could go either to the Magistrates' court or to the County court. However, if you are not married you cannot go to the Magistrates' court for protection. Some solicitors prefer to use one type of court and you should make sure that their choice is in fact the best for you.

County courts have wider powers than Magistrates' courts as to what they can order people to do, or stop doing. For example, they can grant injunctions against harassment as well as actual violence. They may be more willing to grant exclusion orders and less likely to urge reconciliation than Magistrates' courts. They can make orders as part of divorce proceedings against your husband if he is troubling you somewhere away from your house. Magistrates' courts can order payment of lump sums of up to £500 only.

If you live in the country the Magistrates' court will probably be nearer where you live than the County court. It can be useful for getting an immediate court order if you have clear evidence of violence, because it is easier to get legal aid for an emergency application in the Magistrates' court than in the County court. The police will serve the summons or court order on your husband, which can be easier for you, and protection orders may be easier to enforce than injunctions obtained in the County court or High Court. Even if your husband is not arrested when he breaks the order, you can go to the court as soon as it opens and give sworn evidence about what he has done. You can request a warrant of arrest which should result in your husband being arrested very quickly. The magistrates may not be as reluctant to send him to prison for breaking the order as a judge in one of the other courts, provided that you can prove your case.

In the County court and the High Court, the main part of your case will be your 'affidavit', which is a statement that you have written out beforehand and sworn or affirmed before a court officer or lawyer. In all cases, except emergency orders to protect you, your partner will have received a copy of your affidavit and may have sent one in reply. This means that you have time to think about your case and to make sure that you have included all the points you want the judge to consider. Your witnesses can also swear affidavits, and may not have to come to court if their evidence is not disputed by your partner. If you are doing the case yourself it will be necessary to prepare a lot of papers, but you can get help from legal-advice schemes and from the court office to do this. In the Magistrates' court almost all evidence is spoken, so you or your solicitor have to ask for what you want and explain the details of your problem rather than writing it down. Witnesses usually have to come to court, although, to a limited extent, the magistrates may accept written statements as evidence if both you and your partner agree to this. In the County court or High Court, your case will be heard by one judge who will be a lawyer of many years' experience. In the Magistrates' court your case will usually be heard by two or three people who are not lawyers. It is difficult to generalize about what difference this makes – some judges and some magistrates are sympathetic, while others are not. Magistrates' courts do retain the atmosphere of the police courts that they usually are.

The High Court is more expensive than the County court which is more expensive than the Magistrates' court. If you are legally aided the Law Society, which grants legal aid, may ask why it is necessary for you to use the County court, for example, when the Magistrates' court is cheaper. Your solicitor should be prepared to give the reasons why in your case it would be better for the application to be made in the County court.

WHEN YOU APPLY TO THE COURT FOR INJUNCTIONS AND PROTECTION ORDERS

The basic procedure is that you or your solicitor prepares the necessary paperwork, if any, and explains to the court why you are in need of protection. Your address can be kept secret, so you do not have to disclose it, if the court agrees. A date is fixed for the court hearing and a summons or notification of the case is given to the man, together with the court papers. This is called service. However, if you can convince the court that it is an emergency and you need immediate protection, it can be asked to hear the case straight away without your partner being told about it. At the court hearing your evidence and his too, if he is present, is read or heard by the judge or magistrate, who may then make the court orders. Evidence from witnesses may be necessary, either in person or in written statements, and reports from doctors or other professionals. The court expects a man to obey a court order – if he does not he is in contempt of court and may be punished, possibly by imprisonment. It is important to read your court order when you get it, so you know precisely what it says. Injunctions and protection orders are generally valid only when they have been served on the man, but if he was present in court when the order was made, you can still enforce the order, if he breaks it. The injunction or order must be handed to the man personally and its contents explained to him. You should never serve any papers yourself – if you have a solicitor, she will arrange for someone to do this. If you are doing the case yourself, you should arrange for the papers to be served by someone else. The police will serve a summons or order from a Magistrates' court and bailiffs may sometimes be asked to serve County court papers, but they take a long time. You are responsible for getting the papers served on your partner, and if you think that he will get violent when he sees the papers, you can tell the police that you are afraid there will be a breach of the peace and ask them to be present when he is served. They should not refuse to do this, although it may be difficult to persuade them that it is necessary.

IN THE COUNTY COURT

You can use the Domestic Violence Act to apply for a non-molestation injunction, an exclusion order and an order that you are to be allowed to re-enter the home. Under this law, the judge can make a regulatory order which states that you and your partner are to live in different parts of the home. This is unlikely to be a safe solution for you if he is violent. In this court, you can make a claim for trespass and/or assault in order to apply for a non-molestation injunction and an order that he must not come near your home. Or you can commence divorce proceedings and apply for non-molestation and ouster injunctions, an order that he may not come near the home, plus interim custody and maintenance. The paperwork that you will need to prepare varies slightly for the different types of court case. This is an outline of the procedure that you or your solicitor should carry out when applying for a Domestic Violence Act injunction. More information about it can be found in a booklet *How to Get an Injunction.*

First prepare the papers – write out the form of 'originating application'. This sets out your application and states what kind of injunction you are seeking. It lets your partner know that you are applying for an injunction. Your affidavit, a statement which describes the dates, places and nature of any assaults or threats of assaults he has made, is written out. You state in it that you fear you may be assaulted again. If you are asking for an injunction which orders him to leave the home, the affidavit should explain why you cannot continue living in the same house as him and, if possible, what accommodation he can go to. It should also say whether your home is owned or rented in both your names, in his name, or in yours. You have to take the affidavit to a solicitor or court office and swear or affirm that everything in it is true. This is free in some court offices, but a solicitor will charge a standard fee, which can be claimed back from legal aid. It is useful to have written statements from witnesses – people who saw you being attacked or heard you being threatened, or who saw you shortly after an attack when you were upset or injured. They also need to prepare sworn affidavits. You need two copies of each affidavit and three copies of the originating application. It is necessary to apply to the court for your address not to be disclosed if you do not want to write it on the affidavit. Take these papers and a 'draft order' which tells the court which order you want, either to your local County court or to your partner's local court if he lives in a different area. You will have to pay a court fee of a few pounds. Tell the court official that your application is urgent and ask when a judge who can hear the case will be sitting. If a judge is not available soon enough at your court, your application may be able to be heard at another court where a judge is sitting. The court official fixes a date for the hearing not less than five days later and gives you a paper which is called a 'plaint note' with your case number on it. In courts outside London, they may say your case cannot be heard for several weeks, in which case you may be able to use the special procedure for very urgent cases. A judge will not normally grant an injunction if your partner has not been informed of the hearing, unless you can convince him that you need immediate protection and, therefore, your case is very urgent. A copy of the originating application, which is completed by the court official, and a copy of your affidavit should be given to your partner, at least four days (excluding Sunday) before the hearing. Whoever serves the papers on him should complete an 'affidavit of service', saying they have handed them to him personally, confirming the time and place, and saying that he was recognized as the right person. If the papers cannot be delivered into his hands – for instance, if he cannot be found – it is best to leave them at his address, and if he does not turn up at court, ask the judge to agree a procedure for trying to get them to him.

SHORT CUTS IF YOUR CASE IS URGENT

There is no need to wait five days before making an application for an injunction if you ask the judge to grant it in your partner's absence. You can argue that your case is very urgent if you have received injury from your partner and there is danger that he might attack you again, especially if the attack is likely to be serious and it seems too dangerous to notify him of the court case. You can also apply for the injunction to be granted in his absence if he cannot be found. This is an 'ex-parte' application. Normally you can only get an ex-parte injunction which orders him not to assault you. Although you might be able to get an ouster injunction too, it will take a very good solicitor and a sympathetic judge, and you will have to prove that there has been excessive violence or that you have nowhere else to go with the children. It helps if you can suggest somewhere he can go to. Many judges are reluctant to grant ex-parte injunctions at all, although this varies a great deal between one court and another. You may be able to get an exclusion order ex-parte if you are unmarried and he has no legal title to the home. If the injunction is granted ex-parte, a date for another hearing will be fixed, when your partner can attend and put his case to the court. You must be there too. The ex-parte injunction is only a temporary order – until the next hearing – and it will not normally have the power of arrest attached. You can ask the court for a hearing on the same day that you take the papers to court, and you can go to court before preparing all the paperwork or swearing the affidavit, if necessary. Explain the urgency of the situation to the judge and undertake to file all the documents as soon as possible.

The hearing will normally be in chambers, which means the public are not admitted. It will be in open court, however, if you have got to the stage where you are asking for him to be sent to prison. If you have a solicitor, all you have to do is wait until you are called upon to give evidence or answer questions. If you are conducting the case yourself, you can, if you wish, have a non-legal person with you to help you. The judge may suggest that you get a solicitor, but you do not have to do this. It helps if your witnesses are in court, but if that is not possible, you should have their sworn affidavits with you. A doctor's letter confirming that you have been injured is also very useful. Let the judge know that you have witnesses present. The judge will want an explanation of what the application is about. You may have to give evidence, and before doing that you will have to promise to tell the truth either by swearing on a religious book or by affirming (which means the same thing but does not involve a religion). If your partner is in court, he will have the opportunity to ask questions and give his side of the story. If you are asking for an ex-parte injunction, you will have to convince the judge that the case is urgent, or he may adjourn the case and tell you to have your husband notified of it. This means that the hearing is put off for a few days. You can ask the judge to attach the power of arrest to the order she makes, but unfortunately judges are reluctant to do this, which makes court orders very hard to enforce. When the injunction has been written out, it has to be delivered personally to your partner and normally does not become effective until then. If he was in court when it was granted and you cannot find him afterwards, you can ask the judge to enforce it, even though it has not been given to him.

IN THE MAGISTRATES' COURT

Magistrates' courts can grant personal protection orders and exclusion orders to married women only. The rules as to what sort of order can be granted in what circumstances are less flexible than in the County court, and basically come down to these:

1. If your husband has been violent or threatened violence to you or your children, and you or they need the protection of an order, the court can grant a personal protection order telling him not to use or threaten violence. The court can also grant an exclusion order telling him to leave the matrimonial home, when it is satisfied that he has been violent to you or the children, and been violent to someone else or broken a personal protection order, and when it is convinced that you or the children are in danger of physical injury.
2. You can apply for maintenance for yourself if you can prove that your husband has either behaved unreasonably, failed to maintain you or the children, or has deserted you. Even if the court does not find this proved, it can give you custody of the children and order maintenance for them, but not for you.

To get a Magistrates' court order, you or your solicitor should go or write to the Magistrates' Domestic court and explain why you need an order, and what kind of order you need. This is called 'making a complaint'. You make separate complaints if you wish to ask the court for a personal protection order and orders for financial provision, custody and access. The court will issue a summons which has a short explanation of your complaint and a hearing date on it. If you are asking for a power of arrest, this must be stated in the summons, which will then be served on your husband. The hearing will be held as soon as possible, and you have the right to be heard in private. You should have your witnesses with you. Courts are not keen to attach powers of arrest, so you will have to convince the court that you are frightened and do need protection.

In an emergency, when you need immediate protection, the Magistrates' court can grant an 'expedited' order. This means that you get your hearing straight away, and your husband is not served with a summons in advance. If the court grants the expedited order, it is then served on your husband. There are limitations to expedited orders: they are temporary, lasting a maximum of twenty-eight days, which means that you will need to attend another court hearing during that time to apply for a long-term order; and they can be granted only for personal protection, so you cannot get an expedited exclusion order.

IN THE HIGH COURT

You might apply for an injunction as part of defended divorce or judicial separation proceedings. These usually start in the County court and are transferred if your husband defends them. We will describe the procedure in Chapter 6. Wardship proceedings, which we describe later in this chapter, are always held in the High Court and you may apply for injunctions as part of these.

TO CLARIFY THE POSITION REGARDING THE CHILDREN

You do not need to apply for a court order in relation to the children, if you do not want to. There is no reason why you should not take them with you when you leave home or go to collect them when you have found a place to stay. We describe how you can get help in doing this in Chapter 7. You should make sure that you keep them with you when you leave home if you want them to continue to live with you, because their father might win a custody application if he has been looking after them. There is also a danger that you could lose custody if he had kept one child and you kept another, because the courts do not like splitting up families unless they believe that the members of the family separate voluntarily. If they are teenagers, the children may be able to persuade the court that it would be best for them to live with different parents.

It might be necessary for you to apply, as soon as you separate from your partner, for court orders which state who is to look after the children. To do this, you can apply for interim custody, which means that you have the children until a longer-term decision is made about custody. It may be possible to get non-molestation and ouster injunctions where this is in the interests of the children. You can apply in any of the courts, using the Domestic Proceedings and Magistrates' Courts Act, the Guardianship of Minors Acts, or divorce or judicial separation proceedings. Alternatively, in an exceptional case, you can apply to the High Court to have the children made wards of court. If the father has refused to let you have the children, you can get a court order that he must hand them over to you, and he will probably be told not to take them from you again. Custody, access and wardship applications are complicated, and you will almost certainly need the help of a solicitor. As long as you do not have much money, legal aid should not be a problem. Interim custody applications should be heard quickly by any of the courts, generally as part of the injunction hearing. They can, however, complicate your situation, because the father may apply for access when you ask for custody. If he does this and you think he should not see the children, you can try to get the court to agree that it would be better not to make any arrangements for access until the long-term custody order is made, or at least until the ouster injunction is no longer in force or you have been rehoused. It can be very difficult for you to let the father see the children, especially if you are living in temporary accommodation or a women's refuge where he cannot come to visit them. Although courts are reluctant to refuse access orders, even temporarily, you should make sure your solicitor knows if you are unhappy about access and understands your difficulties. If you are worried about problems arising as a result of an access order, you can try to insist that arrangements are made for the access visits to take place in a way that will not put you in danger. Social workers can be asked to supervise the access, by taking the children to see their father in the social services office, for example. The court welfare officer may recommend supervised access, but courts are unwilling to ask social workers to do this because they have too much other work to do. It is important that you do not let the solicitors and courts just agree to access and leave it for you to arrange. If your solicitor thinks you could lose your application for interim custody by refusing access, it may be necessary to work out a way for the man to see the children which will not be too difficult and dangerous for you. We go into the questions of custody and access in more detail in Chapter 6. We also describe how you may be able to appeal if you lose an application for custody. If this happens you should try to keep the children with you until the appeal is heard. Courts can allow the mother to keep the children until her appeal is heard.

WARDSHIP

This is most commonly used when there is a danger that the children might be taken out of England and Wales, because once this has happened it is very difficult to get them back again. If you think the man might snatch the children from you or take them out of the country, you might want the protection offered by wardship, which gives the authorities wider powers to help you than those afforded by a custody order. It is possible to have them made wards of court very quickly, even by telephone in an emergency. Children become wards of court as soon as the completed forms are taken to the court, and you can then request the Home Office to contact ports in order to prevent them being taken out of the country, and also the passport office to tell them not to issue the children with passports without notifying you. If your children are snatched, the court can ask the police to help find them and the DHSS to disclose the address of the man, if he is claiming benefit for them. Wardship is also useful if you are not the children's mother but are concerned about their welfare, for example, with foster children, grandchildren, or nephews and nieces. Once children are wards of court, it is the court who decides where they should live, and any interested person can apply to look after them. In exceptional cases the court can make a local authority responsible for the children by making a care order (this can also be done under the Guardianship of Minors Acts or the Domestic Proceedings and Magistrates' Courts Act). The first wardship order will end after twenty-one days, unless there is an application within that time for it to be continued, and it can be up to a year before the full wardship hearing takes place. The children continue to be wards of court until they are eighteen or you ask the court to end the order, which it can do at any time.

There are disadvantages to having the children made wards of court. The court takes over parental rights, which means that you must consult the court about any major decisions to be taken about the children – for example, if you want to take them abroad or move to another address. You must notify the court if you change a child's school. Children who are wards of court are not allowed to marry or travel outside England and Wales without the court's consent.

If you want to apply for an injunction as part of wardship proceedings, it is necessary to prepare an affidavit and notice of application as in an application for a County court injunction. The court can also make a maintenance order for the children, if you are married to their father, and he may be given access whether you are married or not. During wardship proceedings, children may be separately represented by the official solicitor, whose function is to put their case to the court. As the procedure involved in making children wards of court is expensive, the legal aid authorities are likely to ask why it is necessary to use wardship rather than custody proceedings. Although you can get the Home Office and passport office to assist you when you have a custody injunction, it is a slower procedure.

MAINTENANCE

If you want to apply for maintenance for yourself or the children when you first separate from their father, you can apply for a maintenance-pending suit using matrimonial legislation, and it is also possible to get maintenance for the children in wardship or, if you are unmarried, affiliation proceedings. However, you should consider whether it is in fact beneficial to you to have maintenance, which is discussed in Chapter 6.

PROPERTY

When your relationship ends, you can take with you the possessions you originally had and a share of the property acquired by both of you since you married. The question of who should have the things in the home, if it cannot be decided between you, can be sorted out by your solicitor, or by the divorce court if it is not possible to come to an agreement in any other way. When you go to fetch your possessions, you can ask the police to accompany you in order to prevent a 'breach of the peace', that is, to stop him assaulting you. If he will not let you take what belongs to you or the children, if you are looking after them, the police may be reluctant to interfere. It will then be necessary to get a court order which states which things you can have. You can also get the court to order that he must not sell or destroy any of the property and that he must let you into the home to fetch it. In order to determine who can have the home that you shared, you may have to take out divorce or judicial separation proceedings, which we describe in Chapter 6. Unmarried people who jointly own the house can apply under the Law of Property Act 1925.

WHEN YOU HAVE THE COURT ORDER

It is useful to keep a copy of your court order with you, and also to send one to your local police station to make sure they know about your situation, whether or not you get a power of arrest. When you get an order with a power of arrest attached, a copy of it will be sent to the police, but it is worth you sending them one too. If you think there is a possibility that the man will break the injunction, you should take every precaution possible when returning home. Get the police to accompany you to the place and check that he is not there, if he has been ordered to leave. Change the lock on the door, fix bolts to make it more secure, have a friend to stay with you. It is a good idea to tell the neighbours about the situation, and if you do not have a telephone, ask them either to let you use theirs or to phone the police for you if there is any trouble. Change the routes you take to school and any other places you go alone, if possible. It is obviously difficult to do these things, but you may find that someone can help you, which can make all the difference during the stressful time when you have just taken the step of going to court. Social workers, Women's Aid or advice centre workers may be able to give practical help with things like changing locks, or emotional support if you need to talk to someone. If your partner makes trouble or comes to your home when he has been ordered to leave it, you should phone the police straight away and insist that they come quickly. Explain that you have an injunction and tell them if it has a power of arrest attached. If it is backed by the power of arrest, any police officer may arrest a man if she has reasonable cause to suspect that he has disobeyed the order. It does not matter where you are when the order is broken. The police must have a warrant or copy of the injunction, so be sure you are able to show them yours if necessary. If he is arrested he must be taken to court within twenty-four hours, and you or your solicitor should attend the hearing with your witnesses who can say that he broke the order. So make sure that you find out from the police when the court hearing will take place. If the injunction was not backed by the power of arrest, or if the police refuse to arrest him, you have to go back to court, with your solicitor if you have one, and apply to have him dealt with for contempt of court. In the County court you make an application for committal. Ask for the case to be heard as soon as possible. He must have notice of the date of this new application and cannot be arrested on a warrant. You should prepare a new affidavit saying what he did to break the injunction, which is served on him with a summons to attend court. It helps to have extra evidence to back up your story. If you have a personal protection order without a power of arrest you should go back to the Magistrates' court and apply for a warrant of arrest to be issued. When the warrant has been issued, the police must arrest the man and bring him to court.

You and your lawyer, if you have one, should attend that hearing with your witnesses, and you can take a friend for support.

The judge or magistrate has the power to send your partner to prison, but will do so only if she thinks it is a serious case and if he definitely knew about the injunction. If he is jailed for contempt of court it is a special type of prison sentence which means that he can apply to be released at any time by 'purging his contempt' – that is, by saying he is sorry. You can go to court and oppose his release, but it is up to the judge or magistrate to decide whether he should come out. You have no means, therefore, of knowing how long you will be safe.

HOW LONG DOES A COURT ORDER LAST?

Non-molestation orders from the County court may be valid indefinitely and Magistrates' court protection orders may be made for twelve months or until further notice. A man can be arrested or taken back to court several times using the same injunction. If he goes to prison, the injunction is still effective when he comes out. If you decide that you want to be reconciled while he is in prison, tell the court or your solicitor and the injunction will be lifted so that he can be released. County court exclusion orders were not stated in the Domestic Violence Act to be valid only for a limited period, but have become so as a result of directions given to courts on how to put the law into practice. They are now generally made for a period of three months, but you can go back to court to ask for the period to be extended. Ouster injunctions obtained through divorce proceedings can last until the case is finished and the divorce court can also grant an injunction which continues after the decree, if this is needed to protect the children. Custody orders made under the Guardianship of Minors Acts cease to have effect after you have lived with your partner for six months.

ACCESS AND INJUNCTIONS

If you already have a court order about access which says that the man may come to see the children at your home and you then get an injunction which orders him to keep away from the house, this overrules the access order. He will be breaking the injunction if he comes to your house, unless the injunction specifically allows for him to visit for access. You should not let him in, therefore, no matter what he says about having a right to see the children. If you do let him in you may have problems enforcing the injunction if you need to. The access order can be changed if he is to continue to see the children. You should either ask your solicitor how to alter the terms of access or, if you do not have a solicitor, try to do this yourself by arranging somewhere else for the man to see the children.

6. PERMANENT SEPARATION

I'VE GOT THIS INSANE DESIRE TO KILL MY HUSBAND..!

WHAT LEGAL ACTION SHOULD I TAKE ABOUT MY MARRIAGE OR RELATIONSHIP?

When you separate, you decide what legal action to take, or whether to take any legal steps at all. Solicitors sometimes press a woman to start divorce proceedings because it makes her case easier to deal with – but remember that you employ your solicitor to advise you about your options and represent your wishes, not to tell you what to do. Legal action can be useful to clarify your rights when the marriage ends – who will have custody of the children, where you will live, whether your ex-husband should give you maintenance, and what share of the home and property you are entitled to. Even if you are not married, you may be able to make some claims on your ex-cohabitee in relation to the property you shared and you can ask for maintenance for the children. Here is an outline of the possible types of legal proceedings that you can take.

You can ask the County court for a divorce which ends the marriage, leaving you free to remarry. Maintenance, custody, access and rights to the matrimonial home and property can be sorted out through divorce proceedings. Or you can ask for a judicial separation which ends the marriage on a practical level – you will no longer have a duty to live together or be each other's next of kin, and maintenance, custody, access and property rights can be sorted out – but it does not legally end the marriage. If you are afraid your partner will sell or destroy your personal property or your share of the property acquired since marriage, you can ask the court to order him not to do this as a part of divorce, judicial separation or injunction proceedings. You can make this application early on in the proceedings. In order to prevent him selling the house if it is not in your name, your right of occupation can be registered at Her Majesty's Land Register or at the Land Charges Register.

If you do not want to end the marriage or apply for a share of the matrimonial home you can apply to the Magistrates' court using the Domestic Proceedings and Magistrates' Courts Act 1978 for orders on maintenance, custody and access. Alternatively, either parent, whether or not you are married, can apply for custody of the children or access to them under the Guardianship of Minors Acts 1971 and 1973. This case may be heard in the Magistrates' court, County court or High Court. Under these Acts, grandparents also have a right to request access, although they cannot start the proceedings, and you can make an application for child maintenance if you are married.

If you are not married to the father of your children, you have sole parental rights over them, although he can apply to the court if he wants to have custody or access. Using affiliation proceedings, you can apply for maintenance for the children but not for yourself. However, if you do not want to be financially dependent on your children's father or do not want to go through what could be an unpleasant court hearing, you need not apply for maintenance. Although the DHSS may suggest that you get an affiliation order, they cannot force you to do this. However, if you are on supplementary benefit, they can themselves apply to the court for an affiliation order against your child's father, if they can contact him. In practice, they do not often do this. The procedure through which you can establish what rights you have to the home that you shared are very complex. If it was not in your name, you may still be entitled to a share of what it is worth if you have contributed towards it financially, so it is worth getting advice on this.

OBTAINING A DIVORCE

To start divorce proceedings, you or your solicitor prepares a formal document called a divorce petition, which is a standard form available from a County divorce court. Most County courts can grant divorces, and so can the Divorce Registry at Somerset House in London. You can choose which court to go to. Ordinary legal aid is not available for simple undefended divorce, although your solicitor may be able to do it for you under the green form scheme. Otherwise, it is not difficult to prepare your divorce petition yourself. You may be able to get help, if you are doing it yourself, from law centres or other advice centres, and the booklet *DIY Divorce*, which you can get from County courts, gives clear instructions. If you or your husband do not agree over who should look after the children or how the money and property should be divided, it is best to get advice from a solicitor.

You must have been married for at least three years before you can start divorce proceedings, unless you can show that your situation is exceptionally bad, but this restriction may be reduced to one year in the future. Either you or your husband must have been living in England or Wales for the past year, or be 'domiciled' here, in order to divorce under English laws.

You can get permission to leave your address off the petition form if you need to keep it secret. Fill in details of the marriage, names and ages of the children and which of the five facts your case is to be based on. There is only one ground for divorce – that the marriage has irretrievably broken down – which is proved by one of these five facts:

1. That your husband has committed adultery and you find it intolerable to live with him.
2. That your husband has behaved in such a way that you cannot reasonably be expected to live with him. 'Unreasonable behaviour' includes mental or physical cruelty and rape.
3. That your husband has deserted you for a continuous period of two years or more.
4. That you and your husband have lived separate and apart for two years, and he consents to a divorce.
5. That you and your husband have lived separate and apart for a continuous period of five years or more. His consent is not required in this case.

If you are alleging adultery, the court will expect you to provide some evidence, such as a signed confession from your husband. If he is not willing to sign, it is better to avoid an adultery petition. There is a section for 'particulars' where you set out details of your reason for saying the marriage has broken down. At the end of the form you should state whether you are applying for custody, maintenance and/or a transfer of property order, which means that you are asking the court to transfer the legal title of the home to you. All the children of the family must be listed on the petition, whatever their ages.

You must pay a court fee to 'file' a divorce petition (at present £40), unless you are on supplementary benefit or FIS, or are receiving help under the green form scheme. It must be delivered to the court together with your marriage certificate or a copy of it and a statement of the arrangements you propose for the children of the family, which means any children under sixteen (or who are in full-time education or training) who are children of you both, and any other children who have been treated as children of the family, whoever the biological parents are. You fill in a form answering basic practical questions about the children's health, education, etc., and what arrangements will be made for access. Copies of the forms are sent to your husband with a covering letter explaining what they are and a form to return to the court. This form is called an 'acknowledgement of service' and has two purposes: it proves that he has received the petition, and it gives him the opportunity to state whether he intends to defend the divorce and whether he intends to apply for custody and/or access. If he disagrees with your proposals or applies for custody himself you will be sent a copy of this application.

UNDEFENDED DIVORCE

The procedure for an undefended divorce (where your husband does not disagree with it) is quite straightforward, and the case will remain in the County court. You must prove to the court that your husband has received the divorce petition, so if he has not returned the acknowledgement of service, you will have to arrange for the court bailiffs (or another third party) to hand him another copy of the petition personally. The important point about an undefended divorce is that it is easy. You will almost certainly not have to go to court for the divorce itself, but you will have to go to a court hearing called the 'children's appointment', if you will be looking after them. When the papers are in order, a date is given for the first divorce hearing. You can attend, but you do not have to. The judge deals with cases in batches, and just states that the decree nisi has been granted. When the 'decree nisi of divorce' is pronounced, it means that you are almost divorced, but not quite. If you and your husband agree about the proposals for the children, whoever will be looking after them must attend the children's appointment, which takes place shortly after the decree nisi or just before the judicial separation decree. It is an informal private hearing in front of a judge, at which the judge will read the statement of arrangements for the children, which you filed with your petition, and will probably ask a few questions about schooling etc. The judge will make the custody and access orders if she is satisfied with the arrangements, or the case will be adjourned until another hearing when the questions of custody and access will be determined. If there are no problems with the arrangements for the children, you wait six weeks and one day and then you fill in a form asking for the decree nisi to be made final. This is called a 'decree absolute'. The court will send both you and your husband a certificate of your decree absolute, which is proof that you are really divorced and free to remarry. You will not get your decree absolute until the judge is satisfied that suitable arrangements for the children have been sorted out.

If you and your husband cannot agree about arrangements for the children, a date will be set some time after the decree nisi for a custody hearing, and a judge will decide the matter. If you become involved in a contested custody case, you will need a solicitor to help you prepare it. The judge will hear evidence from you, your husband and witnesses, and will probably order welfare reports to be prepared. If this happens, the hearing will be adjourned until the welfare reports are ready, when the hearing will take place. When welfare reports are to be prepared, you, the children and your husband will be visited by a probation officer or social worker, who will write a report about the suitability of the arrangements being proposed for the children. The completed welfare report is sent to the court, and you can ask to see it. Recommendations made by the welfare worker are usually accepted by the court, but they can be challenged. The judge will consider the report and the evidence and make the custody and access orders which she thinks are in the best interests of the children. As it can take some time for welfare reports to be prepared, the parent who is looking after the children may be given 'interim custody' until the hearing. If custody is contested there may be a long delay before the decree absolute or decree of judicial separation is made.

DEFENDED DIVORCES

Although many husbands say to begin with that they are going to oppose the divorce and 'defend' the proceedings, few divorces are in fact defended, and usually only for tactical reasons. He may find that there are a number of reasons why it is impracticable for him to defend it. You are bound to be able to get a divorce in the end, provided you make out your grounds in the petition – all he can do is delay things. Anyone attempting to defend a divorce will need the help of a solicitor and most solicitors would advise their clients against defending a divorce. If he does decide to defend, it is expensive and it is very difficult to get any financial help from legal aid. Whether or not your husband defends the divorce makes very little difference to what the court decides eventually about the children, money and property, even though these matters will be dealt with by the same court.

If your husband decides to defend the case, it will be transferred to the High Court, and you may become eligible, depending on your means, for legal aid. The case will take a long time – maybe more than a year – and you may have to go through a difficult court hearing to prove the allegation on your divorce petition. However, most divorces are not in the end defended, and if your husband changes his mind about doing this, the case will be transferred back to the County court.

JUDICIAL SEPARATION

To obtain a judicial separation, you do not have to state that the marriage has irretrievably broken down. You just have to prove one of the same five facts as for a divorce petition (see p. 117), and show the judge that you have made suitable arrangements for the children. Judicial separation is useful when you do not want to get divorced or you have not been married long enough to do so, and you want to get the same legal provisions as you would do in a divorce. The procedure is almost the same as for a divorce, but there is only one decree – the decree of judicial separation. You can get divorced after getting a judicial separation.

RELIGIOUS DIVORCE

Where there has been a foreign marriage or a religious ceremony here under different law, which requires a different form of divorce – the Muslim Talaq divorce, for example – the situation is very complex. You should make certain that you get expert advice from a solicitor who has experience in this area of law, and agencies dealing with immigration problems should be able to refer you to someone who knows about this.

CONCILIATION SERVICES

At present, conciliation services exist in only a few places, but in future, they will probably be set up in many areas of the country, and you may well be referred there by the court or your solicitor. They are a new facility designed to help couples to reach mutually agreed decisions about the questions that need to be resolved when they separate (such as custody, access and division of property), before the court hearing, rather than arguing out the dispute in court for the judge to decide on. The courts and legal aid authorities prefer you to use the conciliation service in order to try to reach agreements on these issues, because it is cheaper and easier for them as-well as being considered to be less upsetting for the children. You may be expected to go there only if you are married, or it may be a scheme which deals with either married or cohabiting couples. The type of conciliation service which is operating in your area might be one that you have to go to, or it may be one which you attend voluntarily. In either case, you can take your solicitor with you, and they may want to interview the children too. Anything that is said to the conciliator cannot be repeated in court unless both partners agree to it.

Although conciliation services have been set up with the aim of helping separating couples, it may actually lead to difficulties for you, especially when you have left your partner because of his violence. They will expect you to go for an interview together with him, and may not understand that you do not want to do this because you are afraid of him. However, provided that both you and your partner agree to go to the conciliation service, it is possible for them to see you separately if you can convince them that this is necessary.

There are different types of conciliation services. Some are out-of-court schemes, run by organizations which are independent of the court. You may be referred there automatically, but it is not compulsory for you to go. If you choose not to, it is worth discussing your reasons with your solicitor or Women's Aid group, to make sure that the court does not think that you are just being uncooperative, and so become more sympathetic to your partner's case. This type of scheme may charge a fee, which you might be able to get back from legal aid. The other type of conciliation service, which is attached to the court, does not cost anything and you have no choice about attending if you are referred to it. When there is a disagreement about custody or access, you will be sent to the conciliation service, if there is one, to talk to the welfare officer, who will also talk to your partner, and maybe your children, to see if agreement can be reached. In this case the welfare officer will report to the court, and a consent order will be made describing the custody and access arrangements. Otherwise, a different welfare officer will be asked to prepare a welfare report for the court hearing at which the questions of custody and access are to be decided.

PARENTAL RIGHTS AND CUSTODY OF THE CHILDREN

While you are married, you have joint 'parental rights' with your husband over any children who you both treat as children of the family, whoever the biological parents are. If you are not married, you have sole parental rights over your children; their father has none, although he will gain parental rights if you subsequently marry. If you have not been married, your partner has no rights in relation to the children when you separate, unless he is given orders for custody or access by the court.

Custody consists of two parts: 'legal custody' (called 'custody' in the divorce court) is the right to make most major decisions about the children, for example, which school they should go to. However, if you want to change their surname or take them out of the country you may need your husband's permission, even though you have been granted custody. 'Actual custody' (called 'care and control' in the divorce court) is the right to have the children living with you and it makes you responsible for their day-to-day welfare.

The question of the arrangements for the children is automatically considered when you get a divorce or judicial separation, because you have to provide a statement of arrangements for them with the petition if they are under sixteen, or under eighteen if in full-time education. The court is also obliged to consider the children when it hears your case for financial provision under the Domestic Proceedings and Magistrates' Courts Act, but not when you seek court orders only for personal protection under this Act. When either you or your husband is granted custody of the children, you will also be given care and control of them. It is possible for you to continue to share parental rights with your husband after the decree of divorce or judicial separation, in which case the judge will order joint custody and state who is to have care and control.

If there is a dispute as to who should look after the children when you separate, there are several kinds of proceedings in which you can ask the court to decide who shall have custody, the most commonly used being the Guardianship of Minors Acts and the Matrimonial Causes Act. In any proceedings concerning children, the welfare of the child is the court's 'first and paramount consideration', which means that the judge or magistrate must base the decision on what is best for the children, and the custody decision should not be used to punish either parent. However, the court will not necessarily take into account a child's wishes when deciding who should look after her or him. In exceptional circumstances, the judge may think it is in the interest of the children to make a supervision order, which makes the local authority social services department keep an eye on the care of your children, or a care order, which enables them actually to take over the care of the children. When the court intends to make a care order, the local authority must be notified about this. Once the care order is made, the social workers will decide whether the children live with you, your husband or somewhere else, such as in a children's home or with foster parents.

Custody is likely to be given to you, especially if you have been looking after the children until the case is heard, but there are situations in which women have occasionally lost their applications. This has happened, for example, when they were not rehoused into permanent accommodation, or when the judge believed that they were leading a lifestyle which she considered improper. Your partner may try to persuade the court that you are not a good mother, by making you out to be mentally unstable or implying that you are a prostitute or lesbian, which is a particularly difficult case to fight because of the prejudices courts have against lesbians. You will need an especially sympathetic solicitor if this sort of argument is to be brought up. If you are lesbian, you will have to decide whether or not to admit it, and if you are not going to admit it, you should be absolutely sure that he has no evidence – like letters, diaries or witnesses – that could prove you are. The mere fact that you live with women and go out with them might make the judge take your partner's side. It will mean that you must be very careful after the custody case too, because he can go back to court and apply for custody at any time. Your children, your way of life or friends could all be used against you. If you decide to admit you are lesbian, you can try to persuade the judge that you can bring up the children better than your partner despite your sexuality. Discrediting him as a parent is one way to do this – proving that he is practically and emotionally unfit to look after them. There has been some research done about the care given by lesbian mothers which shows that their children are not set back by the mother's way of life, but it is rare for women who are known to be lesbians to win custody cases in court. You must be careful that the children are not, in the end, taken away from both you and your partner. Although unmarried women do not often lose custody of their children, the father can apply for it and he may win custody in some situations. Again, this is particularly likely to happen if he can produce any evidence that you are a lesbian and so argue that you should not have the children.

Even when you and your partner agree about custody, the court may not approve of your decisions. Judges do not like to split children between parents, although, if they are teenagers, you may be able to persuade the court that it is better for them to be with different parents.

CHANGING A CUSTODY ORDER

If you are refused custody, it may be possible to appeal against the decision of the court, although appeals are not often successful. Your solicitor should ask the court to let the children remain with you, if that is what they have been doing, until the appeal is heard. The case is transferred to a higher court for the appeal. Factors that the court should take into consideration are whether the other court made a decision because of things that are not relevant or whether it failed to take account of something that was important.

It may not even be necessary to fight the appeal case – for example, Ms L. lost custody to her boyfriend in the Magistrates' court because she was living in a refuge. By the time it was to be heard in the High Court she had been rehoused and her ex-boyfriend did not continue with his claim for custody. She had kept the children with her while awaiting the appeal. Some women get their children back in the end even if their husbands do win custody, when the men are only interested in getting at their ex-partners, and do not really want to look after the children.

Another way of regaining custody of your children is by going to court again and making a new application for custody some time later. You can go to court at any time and give reasons why it would be better for the children to live with you than their father. However, the longer they live with him and the more settled they are there, the harder it will be to win this application, unless there are particular reasons why he is an unsuitable parent.

ACCESS TO THE CHILDREN

When a court makes a custody order, custody and care and control of the child will usually be granted to one parent. If this happens, the other parent may want access – that is, to be able to visit the children and take them out, or have them to stay overnight. The courts have a policy that all parents should be allowed regular access to their children unless this would definitely be a bad thing for them. So do not suppose that because your partner is violent he will not be allowed access to your children, or that he is unlikely to get access if you are not married. The parent who is not given custody is usually given reasonable access, and it is often left up to you to make suitable arrangements for the access visits. What is 'reasonable' varies with the circumstances and the age of the child. For a baby it may be one afternoon a month, for a school child it may be one day a week, plus a week or so in the school holidays.

Although you may not want him to have access to the children, it is difficult to persuade the courts that it should not be granted. You have to argue that it is not in the interest of the child to see its father, and solicitors do not often recommend doing this. Only if he has been violent towards the child might he be refused access. Other arguments against it do not seem to have been tried out very effectively in the courts. Solicitors frequently advise that it is best to agree to him having access, so that your application for custody is not made more difficult. You should find out from your solicitor whether there is a possibility that you could lose custody by arguing against an access order, and if this is unlikely, you can say that you do not want him to have it. Reasons that could be given are that the father has a bad effect on the children when they see him, or that the fact that he has been violent towards you in the past will seriously upset them if they have to see him. It might help you to employ independent psychologists or social workers to write a report on the likely effect that access would have on the children, and whether it would physically or emotionally upset them. However, your husband cannot be obliged to cooperate with such an expert, and once proceedings have started, the court must give permission for an expert to interview the children. If they are old enough to decide that they do not want to see your husband, you can ask the court to take the opinions of the children into account, which often does not happen. They can be represented in court by a 'guardian ad litem', a facility for children which, although recognized in theory as a need when their parents get divorced, is rarely even suggested to them. Either parent can request that the children be separately represented, or the judge may decide, possibly on the recommendation of a welfare officer, that a guardian ad litem should be appointed. Someone from the official solicitor's office may then be asked to put their case, or it is possible to have someone like a relative to do it. Separate representation for children is most common in wardship cases, although it may be available for other matrimonial cases.

When children are over ten the court is more likely to take account of their views. A court has been known to refuse access when children have developed such hostility to their father that the court believed that it might be harmful to force them to meet, but such cases are not common. If the father has broken an access order in the past, by not bringing the children back, for example, or by using the visit to assault you, it is more likely that an application for access may be refused, because you can argue that it might happen again. The fact that the father has a criminal record of offences in relation to children or is mentally ill might be accepted as a reason why he should not be brought into contact with the child.

As an alternative to refusing access altogether, you can suggest that he does not have it for the time being, for example, while the ouster injunction is in force, while you are in the refuge or temporary accommodation, or not until the divorce is finalized. Or you can ask the court to grant it on the condition that you do not have to see him or that someone is with you to supervise the visit. It is difficult to get people to make such conditions possible, however, because social workers tend to be too busy, and friends and relatives may not want to get involved. The judge may order that the father can have access as long as it is supervised, but you should make sure that it is not left up to you to arrange this. It is also possible to argue about the extent to which he can have access – that it should not be very often and not overnight. It is helpful if you can sort out the details of access before the custody hearing, if you are not refusing it, and as long as you are not both asking for custody. Solicitors often allow orders for reasonable access or supervised access to be made without going into the practicalities of how it will be organized and who will do it, and you should make sure this does not happen. If you do not want your husband to know where you live or to come into contact with you, you should ask for 'defined access', in which details of how and where he will see the children are made clear at the hearing. There is a great need for a facility to provide supervised access but, unfortunately, no one is prepared to pay for it to be set up. It is possible for the court to enable social workers to supervise the access visits, but they are normally very reluctant to do this and they might just supervise the first few visits and then stop if there are no problems.

CHANGING AN ACCESS ORDER

You can appeal straight away against the court order, which must be done within the time limit. Or you or the father may apply at any time to vary the order. If your partner breaks an access order – if he brings the children back late, for example, or if he uses it as an excuse to assault or pester you – you can try to stop his right to have access. You should then apply to the court which granted the order for his rights to access to be stopped, or for the conditions of access to be changed. He can also apply to court for conditions of access to be changed. If you break an access order, you can be taken back to court by your partner, and you risk being fined or imprisoned, especially if you persist in breaking it. If you want to lessen the rights that the father has to access, it may be easier to do so with an application to vary the order than by appealing, because you must have legal grounds for an appeal other than just your own knowledge that access will cause immense problems. As the courts are reluctant to refuse access, it is, unfortunately, often necessary for you to experience these problems in order to convince the court that access is not a good thing, or that the way in which it is to take place must be redefined.

MAINTENANCE

When you separate from your partner, you may want him to pay some money towards the living expenses of yourself and the children. These payments are called maintenance. He may agree to pay voluntarily, but if not, or if you think that he may change his mind, you may be able to get a court to order him to pay maintenance.

Courts can make maintenance orders in the following circumstances:

1. If you are married and have no children, the court may order your husband to pay you maintenance until you remarry. This depends on how much money you are capable of earning. If you are young and at work, you may not get anything.

2. If you are married and you have the children with you, the court will probably order your husband to pay maintenance for you until you remarry, and for the children until they are seventeen or until they finish their education or training. This depends on how much your husband is earning.

3. If you are not married, you may be able to get an affiliation order against your children's father, which is a finding of paternity and an order that he must pay maintenance for them. However, you cannot get

maintenance for yourself. He could also be ordered to pay a lump sum of up to £500 (at the time the book was written).

4. If you are married and your husband has the children with him, you may have to pay maintenance for him and any children that you have treated as 'children of the family'.

Anyone paying maintenance under a court order can get tax relief on the payments. If you are working or intend to work, you should arrange for orders for your children's maintenance to be payable directly to them, rather than to you, so that you will not be taxed on their maintenance payments.

It is often difficult to decide whether to apply for maintenance or not. Here are some points which may help you decide:

1. If you are receiving maintenance payments already on a voluntary basis, you might as well have the payments confirmed by a court order, especially as there may be tax advantages with court orders. If your husband earns a lot of money, he should be able to afford to pay you and your children enough to live on, so it may be worth applying for maintenance.

2. If you are working or on a low income, or if you intend to start work soon, it is usually worth applying for maintenance.

3. If your husband has a low income and other commitments, he will probably not be able to afford to pay much maintenance, so it may not be worth while applying. If you are on supplementary benefit, you will not gain anything by applying for maintenance unless your husband can afford to pay more than you get from the DHSS, as any money you get will be deducted from your benefit payments.

4. The DHSS may try to persuade you to apply for maintenance, but you do not have to do this. They can, if they wish, sue him themselves for money towards your benefit payments. Many husbands do not keep up maintenance payments, which can be particularly difficult if you are on supplementary benefit and the payments are being deducted from your benefit. You are in a much more secure financial position if you ask for maintenance payments to be made to the court and sent directly to the DHSS, which means that they are not deducted from your benefit.

You may not want to claim maintenance because it is a continuing link with your husband, which may increase the stress you are under if he uses it to get at you or make you financially insecure. Many women prefer to be financially independent, so do not wish to receive maintenance.

HOW TO APPLY FOR MAINTENANCE

If you are married there are a number of ways in which you may apply for yourself and the children. If you are applying for a divorce or judicial separation, you can include a request for maintenance in your petition, which the court will deal with as part of the proceedings. The children's maintenance payments can start at once and yours will begin when you get your decree absolute or decree of judicial separation. If you need maintenance for yourself straight away, you can apply for 'maintenance pending suit', which means payments from the date of your petition to the date of your decree. The court can order periodic payments, which are usually weekly or monthly, and/or a lump sum which is a larger amount of money all at one time. If you are not applying for a divorce or judicial separation, you can apply to the Magistrates' court, County court or High Court for maintenance orders for your children under the Guardianship of Minors Acts. Or you can apply under the financial provisions of the Domestic Proceedings and Magistrates' Court Act, in the Magistrates' court. You can also apply to the County court for maintenance for yourself and your children.

Maintenance Orders from the County Court

You can apply for a maintenance order if one or both of the following conditions applies: your husband has failed to provide reasonable maintenance for you, and/or your husband has failed to provide, or make a proper contribution towards, reasonable maintenance for any child of the family.

The court can order periodical payments or lump sums. Your husband will be asked to state his earnings and how much he can afford to pay.

Maintenance Orders from the Magistrates' Court under the Domestic Proceedings and Magistrates' Courts Act

You can apply for a maintenance order, as well as orders on custody and access, if one or more of the following conditions applies:

1. Your husband has not provided reasonable maintenance for you and/or the children.
2. Your husband has behaved in such a way that you cannot reasonably be expected to live with him.
3. Your husband has deserted you.
4. You and your husband have agreed how much maintenance he should pay you and you want the court to confirm this.

5. You and your husband have been living apart by agreement for at least three months, and he has been making regular maintenance payments which you wish to be continued. The court can order periodic payments and/or lump sums up to £500. Your husband will be asked to state his earnings and how much he can afford. If you have children under sixteen, the court will automatically consider their welfare when you apply for a maintenance order. You will not get it until the court has decided whether it should make an order about custody and access as well.

AFFILIATION ORDERS

If you are not married, the father of your children has no duty to pay maintenance for you and the only way in which he can be ordered to pay towards the children's maintenance is through affiliation proceedings in the Magistrates' court. At the hearing, you must prove to the court that he is their father, and if he denies this, the court may order blood tests to be taken. When you apply for an affiliation order, it is necessary to do so within certain time limits, so it is best to seek advice as soon as you decide that you wish to have maintenance for the children. Affiliation orders usually last until the child is seventeen. The money is usually paid by the father to the court, and the court then pays you or the DHSS. The amount paid for each child varies with how much the father has, but affiliation orders are usually low; he may also be ordered to pay a lump sum.

GETTING YOUR MAINTENANCE ORDER CHANGED OR ENFORCED

Either you or your partner can apply at any time to the court which made the order for a variation, which means having the amount of the payment altered. You should consider applying for a variation if inflation has made your maintenance payments worthless, or your expenses have increased and your payments are no longer adequate, or if your partner's income or circumstances have changed and you think he could afford more.

Your partner may consider applying for a variation, if his income or circumstances change and he can no longer afford the payments, or if you start work or your income increases.

The court will not necessarily vary the maintenance on request; for example, the court should not decrease an already low maintenance order just because your income has increased. If your partner stops sending your maintenance payments, you can ask the court which made the order to tell him to pay up. The court can order that payments be made by 'attachment of earnings', which means that maintenance payments are deducted from your partner's wages and sent to you. Anyone who persistently refuses to pay maintenance ordered by a court can be sent to prison.

THE HOME AND POSSESSIONS

When you leave your partner, there may be questions of property that you want to sort out. This may be personal property, savings, houses and land.

Personal property includes clothes, furniture, household items, cars, etc. It is best to try to come to an agreement with him about who should have ownership of these things, and you may be able to work out such an agreement through your solicitor. But if this is impossible, you can ask the court to make an order as to who should have what. As a general rule, if you are married, half of everything acquired by you jointly since the marriage belongs to you, together with all your own possessions, plus everything you already possessed before you married. Whoever has custody of the children should keep their clothes and possessions. If you are afraid that your partner will sell or destroy the property, you can try to prevent this by applying for a court order restraining him from doing so. If he breaks this order, it is contempt of court, which can be punished by a fine or imprisonment.

Money in your bank, building society or post office account belongs to you, and that in your partner's account to him. If you have a joint account, the money in it belongs to you both equally. This can cause difficulties if you both have individual cheque books, but you can ask the bank to freeze the account until you and your partner have come to an agreement or the court decides how the money should be divided.

Houses and Land are a complicated area of law. If you are an owner-occupier you will almost certainly need the help of a solicitor to sort out your rights to the home. The court can order a variety of solutions depending on whether you own, are buying or renting your home; on who needs it most; and on the amount each of you has contributed to it. Under divorce law, the court has powers to transfer the ownership or tenancy of the property from one spouse to the other, and to decide whether you or your husband should continue to live in it, irrespective of who has the legal title. If you are not married and the home is in his name, you may still be able to get a share of what it is worth, but your right to live in it will depend to a great extent on whether you or your boyfriend is the tenant or owner, because you cannot get it transferred into your name.

While you are married you and your husband both have a right to live in the matrimonial home, whether it is owned or rented in your name or his, unless there is a court order excluding one of you from the premises. If no agreement can be reached between you about who is to continue to live in the home after the divorce or judicial separation, the court can make decisions about the ownership of the property and about the right to occupy it. The divorce court can make a property adjustment order which transfers the ownership or tenancy to you outright, or you can be allowed to live in the home without having the legal title transferred to you. When you decide to claim ownership rights or seek a transfer of property, it advisable to register the fact that you are going to do this (in case your husband tries to sell the home before the legal proceedings are finished), by registering a 'pending action', although this does not have to be done in the case of a tenancy transfer. It is also necessary to register your 'right of occupation', if you intend to continue living in the home when it is not in your name. If you were buying the home on a mortgage which you cannot afford to pay off, but you wish to continue living there, you can make an arrangement with the building society to pay just the interest, which you can get from supplementary benefit, until you can afford to pay off the mortgage. In many cases, the parent bringing up the children is given the right to live in the home until the children finish their full-time education at sixteen or eighteen, when the home will be sold and the proceeds of the sale divided between you and your husband. Alternatively, the court may order that the place is sold immediately and the proceeds divided. Another option that the court has is to make a regulatory order which gives both you and your husband the right to continue living in the house. It states that you should live in different parts of the home.

Unmarried women who own or are tenants of the property can simply evict the man or order him to leave by an ouster injunction. However, joint tenants both have a right to live in a property, and his right to the tenancy can be removed only by persuading him to give it up, which is also the case when he is the tenant. If you are living in a council tenancy which is in your boyfriend's name and he is ordered to leave by an ouster injunction, the council may be able to persuade him to give up his tenancy. However, there is no legal process by which you can remove his right to it. If he owns or is buying the home, it may be possible for you to claim a share of what it is worth. This can be done if you can argue that you contributed to it financially or by making substantial improvements to the property. Your share may not be very much, if anything, especially if you have been there for only a short time or if he has custody of the children. You may, however, be able to establish a right to continue living in the property.

Before you accept a proposed settlement, it is a good idea to discuss with your solicitor what would be the long-term result of the court order. The right to occupy the home until the children grow up, for example, may create housing problems for you in the long term. A half share of the proceeds of the sale of the house may not be enough for you to buy a place of your own, yet you may find that you have no right to be rehoused by the local council, because you have quite a lot of money and you are not in priority need for rehousing. They only have a legal duty to house people who have nowhere to live, if they have children under sixteen, or are old or disabled, unless you can argue that your special circumstances put you at risk if you are not rehoused. If the court suggests that you and your husband live in different parts of the same house, this is likely to be very difficult, especially if he is violent. As an alternative to trying to get the right to occupy the matrimonial home or to a share of the proceeds of selling it, you can apply to the council for rehousing when a marriage or relationship ends. However, this is only possible if you cannot get enough money to buy a place of your own, and if you have the children, or are old or sick. The ways to go about approaching the council or other places where you can seek help are described in Chapter 3. We also describe how you can get a new home from the council or a housing association by getting them to transfer you to another property, in which case a transfer of tenancy through divorce proceedings is of use to you. If this is what you intend to do, it is advisable to find out whether this will be possible and how long it will take before you try this course of action. You can get advice from your local Women's Aid group or an advice centre. The question of where you can stay while you wait for the divorce proceedings to be finished, if it is impossible to stay in the matrimonial home, is also likely to cause problems. Although you may be able to stay in a refuge or in temporary accommodation provided by the council, if you have to leave home because of domestic violence, the length of time it takes to complete divorce proceedings may mean that it is better to apply for rehousing instead.

7. LEGAL RIGHTS AND YOUR CHILDREN

When you first think about ending your relationship and possibly leaving home, either for a while – to have a break and think about what to do – or with the intention of setting up a new one elsewhere, you may feel that you should not do it because of your children. You may be afraid that you could lose them or that the change would be too great an upset for them. There will undoubtedly be changes for them to cope with. They may have to change schools and leave their friends and neighbourhoods as well as their home and possessions, and they will have to live without their father, probably in temporary accommodation for a time. They will, however, be out of a violent or tense domestic situation, in which they too may have been confused and hurt. The relief that this brings generally outweighs the disruption in their lives. You need to get the confidence to trust your feelings about what is best for you and them, and not be discouraged by people who may tell you that it is better for a family to stay together, even when you are subjected to cruelty and violence. Some people you will meet will say that children are deprived if they do not have a father at home, or that major changes in lifestyle should be avoided. But others will support your action. The courts generally allow a mother to continue to look after her children after separating from a violent man, and there are places where you can go for help if you do decide to live on your own with the children. You are entitled to money from the DHSS if you have no income or your wages are low, although they do not give you very much, and social workers might help you out in an emergency by giving you some money or vouchers for food if you have none. If you have children, the local council housing department have a legal duty to give you a place to stay, if you are homeless. It is possible to get the children into new schools straight away where the staff should be sympathetic to your situation. If you decide that it would be in the interests of the children for them to stay with their father or live with other relatives, you may need help in making the arrangements for access, so that you can see them regularly.

In this chapter we go into the ways in which you can use the law and social facilities to help you and your children. However, you may find that the authorities are not very helpful or sympathetic when you approach them, so you will have to persevere with your claims for assistance, and seek out people who are able to give you good advice and back up your case. We also explain how in certain circumstances, although these are rare, you could lose your right to bring up your children. In describing how problems can arise we try to show you how they can be avoided or, with a bit of help, solved.

When you separate from your partner, the situation is more complicated if you have had children by him. It is necessary to consider straight away whether you want to bring them up yourself, and if you do, it is usually best to keep them with you, wherever you stay, until you have been to court or are rehoused. If their father decides to apply for custody, he has a better chance of getting it if he has been looking after them for a while, because courts are sometimes reluctant to move children who seem to be settled somewhere. If you cannot take them with you when you leave home, you can go to collect them when you have found a place to stay. It is advisable not to do this on your own if it might be dangerous; you can ask friends, relatives or workers from Women's Aid refuges who may be able to help you. You can request the police to be present when you fetch the children, which they should not refuse if you explain that there is a danger that there will be a 'breach of the peace'.

GETTING LEGAL HELP

The police may just watch while you fetch the children and make sure you or they are not assaulted. If their father will not let you take them, the police might try to persuade him to let you do this, or they might not want to get involved. Police attitudes vary greatly in such situations and it is generally hard to get them to help when they do not want to. Some believe that the children should be with the mother, especially when they are very young, while others do not like to interfere in a family situation unless there is a court order. As an unmarried mother, you have sole parental rights over them, which in theory means that you can take the children with you wherever you want to, but in practice it may be more difficult. If you are married, it may be necessary to get a court order stating that you have the right to care for the children, before the police will help. While you are married, you and your husband have joint parental rights over any children whom you have both taken responsibility for bringing up, whoever the biological parents are. Only a court order can legally force him to hand the children over to you. It may be easier to avoid a direct confrontation by collecting the children from school or leaving home with them while he is out. If it is necessary for you to establish a legal right to care for the children, there are a number of types of court proceedings which you could choose.

LEGAL PROTECTION, CUSTODY AND WARDSHIP

If you think your partner might try to prevent you from taking care of the children when you separate, either by applying for custody or by snatching them from you, it is advisable to get a court order giving you custody. This can be done when you first leave by making an application for interim custody, which we describe in Chapter 5. You can get an injunction as part of these proceedings, ordering him not to harm you or the children. If he will not let you have them, you can ask the court for an order that he returns them to you.

When you are afraid that he might snatch them, you may either apply for interim custody and an injunction which forbids him from taking the children, or you can have them made wards of court, a legal process which is usually done when it is necessary to act quickly in order to protect the children. We described how children are made wards of court, and we also went into the disadvantage of wardship, in Chapter 5. If there is a danger that they might be taken out of the country, wardship may be a faster and more effective deterrent than custody and injunctions. Once the children are wards of court, the court is responsible for their care and it will decide who should look after them. When the emergency is past, you can apply to end the wardship. While they are wards of court, no one is allowed to take them out of England and Wales without the court's permission. If the children are taken from you, the Home Office will contact the ports in order to prevent them being taken out of the country, and the passport office to tell them not to issue the children with passports without notifying you. You can also ask the Home Office and passport office to help if you have an injunction ordering him not to remove the children, and in cases which are not likely to result in international kidnapping, an injunction would probably be sufficient. The High Court can make a 'seek-and-find' order, if it is necessary to search for your children, which is enforced by someone called the 'tipstaff', with the help of the police.

When you think your partner might apply for custody, it is a good idea for you to confirm that you have the right to bring up the children, by getting custody. We described the types of proceedings through which custody applications are made in Chapter 6. Although custody is generally given to the mother, your partner can also apply for it whether you are married or single, and you cannot rely on getting custody just because you have normally looked after the children or because he was violent towards you. It helps to keep the children with you after you separate from him, because it is harder, though not impossible, to win an application for custody when they have been living with him for some time. If you decide that they should continue to live with him, you can use the same procedure to apply for access. You may prefer to take no legal action in relation to the children if there is no disagreement between you and their father as to who should take care of them and there is no danger that he could at some time get custody instead of you. In some circumstances, legal action could just complicate your situation, because it is likely to result in access being granted to your partner, through which he will be able to keep in contact with you.

ACCESS

It is common for courts, even when they give custody to the mother, to grant access to the father, because it is generally thought to be better for children to be in contact with their father. When you apply for interim custody, custody or wardship, the court is likely to give your partner access. Even if the children do not want to see their father, the court may decide that it is in their interest to do so and make an access order. We describe what rights children have to put their views to the court later in this chapter, though their right to representation does not ensure that the court acts on their wishes. The question of whether a violent or aggressive man should have access to his children is very complicated and the courts often ignore any feelings that you may have about it – such as the fear that he may not bring the children back, or that he will be able to find out where you live and assault you. Although you can argue against access, it is hard to get a court to refuse it unless your partner has abused it in the past. We do not think you should have to be subjected to additional pressures or distress in order to prove your point about an access order, but unfortunately this is often necessary. We went into the arguments you can use against access and

how you can attempt to end an order that has been made in Chapter 6. The court is more likely to be willing to define exactly how and where the access visits should take place, than to refuse an application for access. However, the authorities are reluctant to provide the help that you might need in arranging visits in a situation that would be safe for you. The way to ensure that access is not used by your ex-partner to find and harass you is for someone else to take the children to see him in a place away from your home and bring them back again. If your family and friends do not want to get involved, you need an independent service to provide supervision of access visits. Social workers could be asked to do this, but they are generally unwilling because they have too much other work.

INTERNATIONAL RIGHTS IN RELATION TO YOUR CHILDREN

Once children have been taken out of this country it is very difficult to get them back. Wardship can be used to prevent children being taken abroad, but once they have gone, even if they are wards of court, it is generally necessary to go to that country and use the laws there to try to get them back. It is sometimes possible to use wardship to get back children who have been sent or taken abroad. Whether you will be successful in bringing them back to England will depend on the type of divorce and custody laws that are practised in the country they have been taken to. It is best to get advice from someone who specializes in this area of law, which you can get free if you are eligible for the green form scheme, or some legal advice centres may be able to help.

HOUSING

The Housing (Homeless Persons) Act gives a local authority a legal duty to provide housing for people with children who are homeless, which is explained in Chapter 3. If it is not safe for you to stay in your home with the man excluded from it, you can apply to the local authority for rehousing, although you may need legal advice and support in enforcing this right. You may be told that you have to get a divorce or a custody order before they can help, in which case it is advisable to get help from Women's Aid or a lawyer, because you do not necessarily have to do this. When you apply for custody you are more likely to win the case if you can reassure the court that you will have a place in which you can live with your children.

LEGAL AID

Legal aid is available for custody or wardship cases if you are living on a low income or welfare benefits and do not possess many savings. If you own property and it is ever sold, you may have to pay back the legal aid. The legal aid authorities prefer to give you legal aid for a custody application than for wardship which is more expensive. But there are some circumstances in which your solicitor can insist to the legal aid authority that it is necessary to make the children wards of court, such as when you know that their father plans to take them out of the country. The other situation in which you might need legal aid is when your right to bring up your children is threatened by care proceedings and the court may order that the responsibility for their care is given to the local authority. You can get legal aid to employ a solicitor who will represent the children, and this will generally mean that she will represent you too, but if she disagrees with you, it will be necessary for you to make a separate application for legal aid in order to employ another solicitor to represent you. Free legal advice and assistance about cases concerning children is available from some advice and law centres, the Family Rights Group and the Children's Legal Centre, whose addresses are given in Appendix I.

THE ROLE OF SOCIAL WORKERS

Social workers have various legal powers and duties in relation to children. If they believe that children are in potential danger, they must try to prevent anything happening to them, which means that they ought to help you with any problems that arise when you leave home with your children. However, approaching social workers can lead to difficulties, if they believe that you are not able to look after the children yourself, and decide that they ought to go into care. Social workers' attitudes vary greatly depending on the types of local authority who employ them as well as their own views. Some might be very helpful, while others may try to persuade you to return to the violent man or start talking about putting your children into care when that is not what you wanted to do.

Social workers have the power to get you money if you have none in an emergency. They can pay for you to stay in a bed-and-breakfast if you have nowhere to go, or they can help you to find a place to stay, by ringing up refuges, for example, or by pressurizing the Housing Department. If you are having trouble getting accepted for rehousing by the council, social workers can back up your application, if they believe you should be given sympathetic treatment due to your circumstances. They might also help you to fetch your children, if you could not take them with you. If you want a nursery place for a child, a social worker is best able to arrange this. They may be willing to try to raise money from charities to pay off debts. In some circumstances, they may accept children into voluntary care at your request. However, their reponse to this will depend on a variety of factors apart from your wishes. They may agree, if they know you and believe the children will be better off in care, or if you have a particular problem which will make it impossible for you to look after them temporarily, such as physical bad health, depression, or the birth of a baby. Otherwise, they are more likely to suggest that you get family help, a nursery place, or some other support which will enable you to continue looking after them. However, there is a possibility that once the social workers agree to take the children into voluntary care, they may be reluctant to let you have them back when you feel able to look after them again, although they may not inform you of this at the time. Putting the children into voluntary care can make the social workers think about whether they would be better off in the permanent care of the local authority, especially if it has been for longer than six months.

THE DANGER THAT YOU MAY LOSE YOUR CHILDREN

When you separate from your partner, you could lose your rights to bring up your children, either by losing custody of them to their father, or by the court deciding that neither you nor he should be responsible for looking after them. Their father could either make an application for custody or have them made wards of court and get the court to give him care and control of them. Although this does not happen very often, some men are able to appear convincingly well behaved to anyone in authority. You may, therefore, need some back-up in showing the court that he would not be a good father, which is why it is best not to hide the fact that you have had problems with him from people like doctors and social workers. We described what can happen in custody applications in Chapter 6. Remember that you can appeal against a court decision and a higher court may reverse the first court order, but it is not easy to win an appeal. While you wait for an appeal to be heard, it is best to keep the children with you, so your solicitor should ask for you to be given interim custody until the appeal.

The other way in which you could lose the children is by a decision of the court that neither you nor your partner should continue to look after them. A judge, when considering an application for custody or wardship, can decide that neither of you should have the children, and make a care order. This makes the local authority responsible for the care of the children, and social workers will decide where they should live and who they should see. However, it is not common for an application for custody to result in a care order, especially when you are leaving a violent home in order to set up a better one for you and your children. If it is likely that a care order could be made as a result of wardship proceedings, the children can get independent advice and representation during the court case. When a care order is made by the High Court, it can direct the social workers to give you access to the children, although this need not be frequent.

When welfare workers, the National Society for the Prevention of Cruelty to Children or the police believe that you should no longer be responsible for the care of your children, they may apply to the Juvenile court for a care order, pass a resolution taking over parental rights or ask the High Court to make the children wards of court. If the care order is made by a court other than the High Court, it cannot give any direction about the children's upbringing or access requirements. However, under the Health and Social Services and Social Security Adjudication Act 1983, you will be able to apply to a Juvenile court for access to children in care. A care order is not often made because of a decision to leave the man you were living with, but it is as well to know what they can do and how to try to prevent it from happening. The decision to put children into care is usually based on reports from people like health visitors, doctors or teachers, who will contact social workers if they think a child is not being cared for properly. Very often all the people who have had some dealing with a child will be asked to meet at a 'case conference' to discuss whether a care order is necessary. You do not have the right to be present at such a meeting. Legislation relating to children, as well as public opinion, puts a duty on social workers to interfere when they think children might be in danger. It is difficult for parents to argue against applications for care orders, and even harder to end the care order once it has been made, against the wishes of a social work department. You should, therefore, get advice from someone who you can be sure is knowledgeable about this area of law and is sympathetic to your situation, as soon as you think there is a chance that the children might be taken into care. You may be able to prevent it from happening by satisfying the social workers that there is no need for them to intervene in this way. Their worries about the welfare of the children may arise from problems that you can solve with some good advice and help, or they may be the result of wrong assumptions that the child is at risk.

You should not assume that you must stay in a violent home in order to prevent the children being taken into care: it is better to get help in sorting out your housing or legal rights. Unfortunately, social workers sometimes put more effort into taking children into care than helping their parents sort out problems, and social workers are often reluctant to let you know what they are going to do or the reasons for doing it.

WAYS IN WHICH CHILDREN ARE TAKEN INTO CARE

VOLUNTARY CARE

You can ask the local authority social services department to receive your children into voluntary care if you are not able to look after them for the time being, or a social worker may suggest that you do this. In most cases you can simply ask and you will be able to take your children back home, but there are some circumstances in which this may be difficult. If they have been in care on a voluntary basis for more than six months, you must give twenty-eight days' notice that you want to take the children back. During this time, the local authority can begin the procedure that prevents you from doing so, although it is only in exceptional circumstances that they will want to do this. They can either apply to the High Court for the children to be made wards of court, or they can 'pass a resolution' which gives them the power to take over parental rights from you without going to court.

RESOLUTION FOR PARENTAL RIGHTS

The social workers write a report recommending that the resolution is passed by the social services committee, and they may ask you whether you object to the resolution before the committee considers it. Otherwise, they must write and tell you about it afterwards. You have one month in which to write and say you object. If you do this the local authority must apply to the Juvenile court for the resolution to be continued and, depending on your income and savings, you can get legal aid to fight this court case. The local authority must convince the court that it has good reason for wanting to take over parental rights of your children, and if it does not prove its case you will be able to take the children home. Either you or the local authority can appeal to the High Court against the court's decision, and this must be done within twenty-eight days.

WARDSHIP

Alternatively, the local authority may apply to the High Court for the children to be made wards of court. This might be done when you have put them into voluntary care and you want to take them home again but the social workers do not think you should do this. The court would be asked to make the children wards of court and to give the responsibility for their care to the local authority. This would continue until the court brings the wardship to an end.

CARE PROCEEDINGS

The legal process by which the Juvenile court orders your children into the care of the local authority may be started in two ways. In an emergency, when social workers think children might be in danger and should, therefore, be removed from their parents, they can ask a magistrate to agree to make a 'place-of-safety' order. This can last for up to twenty-eight days. They do not have to go to court for it and, once the order has been made, there is little that you can do except prepare to fight for your children to be returned when the applications for an interim care order or the full care order are heard. The social workers should let your children go home when the place-of-safety order finishes, unless they want to keep them in care, in which case they should apply to the court for a care order before the place-of-safety order expires. But if they are not ready to put their case to the court, or if you have not had time to get legal help, the court can make a series of 'interim care orders', each of which lasts for up to twenty-eight days. It is also hard for you to prevent these orders from being made, which means that your children could be kept in care for months before the court hears the case for making a care order. However, you should discuss with a solicitor the possibility of arguing against the interim care orders. The police can also keep children in a place of safety for up to eight days without getting an order from a magistrate.

If the situation is not considered to be an emergency, the local authority social workers, police, or education welfare officers will apply to the court for a hearing at which it will be decided whether a care order should be made. You will receive a summons to go to court. The case will be heard by magistrates who specialize in cases concerning children, and if you want to dispute the care proceedings you can do so on your own or employ a solicitor. If there is a difference of opinion between you and the solicitor as to what is in the interest of the children, it is their case that the solicitor should put to the court and you can employ another solicitor to represent you. Otherwise, you can tell the court what you think without having a solicitor to represent you. The magistrates will hear all the evidence and then they generally ask for a welfare report to be prepared by the local authority social workers. This is generally available only on the day the case is heard. You and the children must be told of anything in the report which is important to the case, and you can challenge this in court, but they do not have to show you the report.

ARGUMENTS AGAINST A CARE ORDER

It is a good idea to make a big display of your concern about your children, and it is a good idea to visit them while they are temporarily in care before the case is heard. In order to do this, you contact the social worker and ask for a visit to be arranged, although they can refuse if they want to. Your solicitor should try to find out what reasons and evidence the local authority is going to give for requesting a care order. You can employ your own social worker or psychologist to prepare a report on whether they think a care order is necessary, and to give evidence in court if they think it is not. In some cases they can be paid by legal aid. The witnesses that speak in court in favour of the care order should be cross-examined in order to find out whether they do, in fact, have any proof that the order is necessary. Reasons for granting a care order are that a child is being, or might be, ill treated, neglected or exposed to moral danger; or that the children are beyond parental control, are not receiving education or have committed an offence. In addition, the court must be shown that the children are in need of care or control. If the court order is being sought because of particular problems that you have, you may be able to solve them before the order is made. Hassle the local authority for housing if you are homeless, get help in working through emotional upsets. If the children are at risk from their father, the fact that you leave him should be enough to remove the threat of a care order.

WHAT ORDER CAN BE MADE

A court can refuse to make any order. It can ask whether you will promise to 'exercise proper control' over the children for a period of up to three years, and if you do not look after them in the way the court considers proper, you could have to pay a sum of money which is fixed by the magistrate. It can place the children under the supervision of the local authority for a fixed period of time up to three years. This means that a social worker or probation officer has a duty to visit and to advise and help you if necessary. The children may also be told to live with a particular person, to stay away from home for a period to take part in 'intermediate treatment', or to have treatment for a mental condition if they have agreed to it. And the court can make a care order, which makes the local authority responsible for the children's upbringing until they are eighteen or nineteen, or until the order is brought to an end. The local authority can allow children who are in care to live with you or the father, or place them with foster parents or in a children's home. It should take account of the wishes and feelings of the children, but does not always do so. It should be possible for you to have access, and you can argue for this to be arranged or ask the court to allow you access.

WHEN CHILDREN ARE IN CARE

When children are in care, you do not have any right to say how or where they should be brought up, although the court can order you to pay towards the upkeep of the children if you can afford it. If you do not keep on good terms with the social worker it is especially difficult, because you cannot demand frequent access to your children, although they may allow it, and they can help you pay for the visits. They should review the case every six months and consider whether to apply for a discharge of the care order. As social workers generally have the intention of keeping families together, and should take the wishes of the children into account, they ought to involve parents and children in these reviews, but they tend not to, and there is little you can do about this. Although it is very hard to keep up your relationship with your children when they are in care, it can be very difficult to get them back if you do not. Social workers can allow them to live with you at any time, and that is much more likely to happen if you have kept up regular contact. If you are not able to visit you should write letters. If you do not get on with the social worker, it is unlikely that the local authority will arrange for a different one to take over the case. You can get advice and help from other agencies like Women's Aid or advice centres, who can talk to the social worker on your behalf. Either you or the social workers can apply to the court for a care order to be changed or ended, and legal aid is available for this.

ENDING A CARE ORDER

When a care order has been made, or your parental rights have been taken away by a resolution passed by the local authority, you may either appeal against it or apply to the Juvenile court to have it 'discharged' or 'varied'. In the case of a care order, you or the children can make these applications and you would get legal aid to pay for a solicitor. The notice of appeal must be sent to the court within twenty-one days of the care order being made, and then the whole case is heard again in the Crown Court. If you can convince the appeal court that the other court came to the wrong decision, the care order will be dropped, but it is not easy to do this. Alternatively, you can apply at any time after the order was made to have it discharged or varied. Subsequent applications cannot be made at less than three-month intervals. These applications are also difficult to win, but it is worth trying. If you can show that the original reason for making the care order no longer exists, the court can end it, but it does not have to, if the magistrates think it is in the interest of the children to remain in care. However, the social workers may agree that a care order is no longer necessary and not oppose the application, or they can apply to the court to end it themselves. A court can discharge a care order and make a supervision order instead, if that seems more appropriate. You can appeal against a court's decision not to discharge or vary an order in the same way as you appeal against the order being made in the first place.

CHILDREN'S RIGHTS TO HELP AND REPRESENTATION

When you separate from the father of your children, the decision about who they are to live with and whether they should see the other parent may be quite problematic for them. If they need help, either before or after you split up, there are agencies which aim to assist the children in understanding and coming to terms with what is happening, and in expressing their opinions about it. However, the resources which children can use to get help and representation of their opinion vary greatly in different parts of the country, both in availability and in the attitude of the people working in them to the idea of rights for children.

LEGAL REPRESENTATION

Within the legal system, attitudes are confused about the question of children's rights. Although the decisions made by the courts in matrimonial or care cases are supposedly based on what is best for the child, children are not given much opportunity to express their opinions, and the decisions made may be precisely what they have said they do not want. When a care order is applied for, the children can have their own lawyer, but when a local authority applies for parental rights, no representation is available for children. The language in which their futures are discussed is hard for anyone but professionals to understand, and many solicitors have not learnt much about legal work involving children, let alone how to discuss the case with the children concerned. Although legal representation is available for children in wardship proceedings, if the case is thought to be difficult or complicated, or when a care order might be made, they are not often informed of this and the facility is rarely used. A 'guardian ad litem' is a person who represents children in a matrimonial case. She or he is likely to be a social worker, in the Juvenile court or County court, but is more likely to be the 'official solicitor', a lawyer who works for the courts, in the High Court. Someone from the official solicitor's department will visit the children to find out from them what they think should happen, and also talk to you and get reports from places like their school. A report is written for the court which recommends what seems to be best for the children, and they can ask the official solicitor to tell the court if they disagree with the recommendation. When children would like to see their father, but it would be very difficult for you to arrange access, the guardian ad litem can ask the court to order supervised access and insist that practical arrangements are made for this to happen.

THE CONCILIATION SERVICE

Conciliation services exist in only a few areas of the country at present, although they will probably become more widely available in the future. Their function is to help families sort out problems caused by parents separating, by acting as mediators in discussions between the partners over the areas of disagreement such as custody, access and property. The authorities prefer you to use the conciliation process as a means of solving conflict because it is considered to be less upsetting for the children, as well as being a cheaper and more effective way to sort out practical problems than a contested court hearing. The conciliation service workers may wish to interview the children as well as you and your partner. There are two types of conciliation service, which we described in Chapter 6. You do not have to go to the out-of-court schemes, but you have no choice about attending the type of scheme which is attached to the court. This may create difficulties, because they generally expect you to go for an interview together with your partner, which you may be afraid to do. It will be necessary for you to explain that you left him because of his violence, and try to convince the conciliation service workers that they should not insist on seeing you together. It may help to ask Women's Aid workers or your solicitor to discuss this with them, and if you go to the conciliation service you can take your solicitor or someone else for support.

The service may be useful in sorting out access arrangements. As the court is unlikely to refuse your partner access, it may be helpful for you to try to work out a way in which the children could see their father which does not mean that you have to see him. You could ask the conciliation service to suggest arrangements which would make this possible, although it does not, unfortunately, have any power to make the court order supervised access.

INCEST

Although incest is not widely talked about, it is quite common in our society. Research shows that a large number of children are subjected to sexual molestation by men they trust or who are in a position of authority. Far more girls experience sexual assault than boys, usually from a man or older boy who they know, and often in the home. The girls may be any age, one reported case being with a nine-month-old baby, but girls between the ages of eight and fifteen are most at risk. The man often makes excuses, saying the girl was willing or that it was his wife's fault, but incest and sexual assault on children are serious crimes and have a damaging effect on the children that lasts into adulthood. They often cannot stop it for fear that they will not be believed if they tell anyone, or that this may have disastrous repercussions. If you suspect that anything like this is happening to your daughter, it may well be true, and the advice given by women and girls who have survived incest is that the best course of action is for mother and daughter to talk about it. This is very difficult, because the man is likely to impose rules of silence on the child, and use threats or bribery to enforce this. It may help to let her know that you think she might be having problems and talk about troubles you have had with him too. She might feel unable to tell you about it because of the difficulty that it could create for you. He might have said that it would cause the family to split up if you knew about it, and this could be true. When you talk to your daughter about what is happening, she will want to know how the abuse can be stopped, and the answer will vary with the circumstances. Just challenging him about his behaviour might cause him to stop, but in many cases it is necessary to take legal action against him or make sure your daughter no longer lives with him. She will need reassurance that it is not her fault and that you will support her through whatever process is required to end the situation.

It is very hard to bear the responsibility for dealing with the situation on your own, and difficult to get the sort of help that you need. Social workers should inform the police, although many will just suggest family therapy or send your daughter to see a child psychologist. You may not wish to enter family therapy or you may feel that something more effective must be done to ensure that you and your daughter are safe from the man who is causing the problem. Sometimes social workers decide that the solution is to take the child into care, especially if your daughter runs away from home because of the abuse and she is under sixteen. The police may or may not be helpful, depending on the attitude of the individual policeman or woman you talk to. They are supposed to investigate the alleged offence, which will involve questioning your daughter and a medical examination, but the case may not reach court.

As there has been a lack of effective help with incest, women are beginning to set up organizations in many places which can give more sympathetic advice and assistance. Rape Crisis centres deal with all forms of sexual assault, on children as well as adults, and you can telephone at any time to ask them for advice. You can contact the Incest Survivors Campaign who can put you in touch with other mothers who have been in the same situation, or suggest solicitors, doctors, therapists or social workers who are likely to understand the problem. They hope to set up an advice centre to give both mothers and daughters support in tackling incest. These organizations can help you find a place to stay if you need to get away from the man who has committed the assaults. The Incest Survivors Campaign plan to set up refuges for girls who need to get away from sexual abuse at home, and there are some hostels for young women which give support to girls in this situation. If you wish to leave home with your daughter, you can both go to stay in a Women's Aid refuge.

There are a number of things that you can do, but you are likely to need a lot of support in challenging incest, whichever option you try. You can get an injunction on behalf of the child to get the man out of the home, or to keep him out of certain rooms in it, although there may be problems in enforcing this type of court order. Alternatively, you can apply to the council to be rehoused where he cannot find you. You should have no problem in getting immediate custody, provided that you are not disbelieved. He may be prosecuted by the police when you make a complaint to them, in which case they will call you as a witness. The trial could be long and distressing for both you and your daughter. You will be cross-examined by his lawyers, who will probably try to make you seem responsible for what he has done, and she may have to give evidence. If he is found guilty, his sentence is likely to be two years' imprisonment at the most. One of the biggest problems that you or your daughter may face is the reluctance that the people who could help you have in believing that sexual abuse has happened. However, it is important that women do not just let this sort of assault continue because it is so hard to challenge, which is why there are many groups being set up all over the country to enable us to help one another to do something about sexual assaults in the home.

8. LIVING AS A SINGLE PARENT

Moving into a new home on your own or settling into your old home without your partner can be very difficult. You have made a decision which has changed your life dramatically. When you first leave, you have housing, legal proceedings, money, solicitors and maybe continuing feelings of fear and anger to occupy your mind. When you finally settle down with at least some of these things sorted out, you will be faced with a period of adjustment, getting used to living without a partner, most probably on your own with your children. If you have lived with a man who took no part in child care, you will not necessarily notice his absence in this respect. But there is certainly a feeling of greater responsibility, in that you are alone and the children can depend only upon you for emotional and financial security. Leaving home is usually very traumatic for the children too. They need to know what they are doing and it is important to tell them what is happening, not necessarily in much detail, but at least so that they know where they are going. It is easier to tell them the truth: that you are not returning home or that you don't intend living with your partner any more. You should also be prepared for them to demand more of you during this time, as they will be keen to hold on to what remains of their security. Children are very adaptable, and if they know and understand what is happening, they will settle down much more easily. They need a period of adjustment as well, in order to get used to having only one parent instead of two, so you should allow them some space in which to get used to the idea. The likelihood is that if the man was violent, your children will be happier outside that situation and will adapt readily to their new life.

Starting life as a single parent can be made more difficult by the added pressure of continuing legal proceedings. A divorce can take years to complete and it is possible that you will be in a new home, or resettled in your old one, before it is finalized. You may have to attend court hearings, and you will probably still have some contact with your husband, however slight. Eventually, with assistance from advice agencies, Women's Aid or a sympathetic solicitor, you will come to the end of the legal process.

The feeling of added responsibility will probably be tinged with a sense of relief, if you have been in a violent and oppressive relationship – there will always be advantages to ending such a relationship.

> 'I have three sons aged eight, four and two which I am bringing up on my own. When their dad and me split up it was hard – not only did I have to cope on my own, as I went into the refuge, I had to cope with living with other families as well. Anyway, we got by and at least I had someone to talk to in the evenings about the problems the day had brought. The most common one being the Giro hadn't come as promised, but you got by, well you had to. Anyway, we then got a place of our own. I was delighted, it seems like we had finally got there. After months of living with other people I finally had my own front door. Everything in life seemed great. After a couple of weeks the novelty of your own place wears off. I didn't know anyone in the area I was living, I had no one to talk to in the evenings when the kids were in bed. The only people I knew were in the refuge. I did have a telly but after a while that gets on your nerves. How social security say it is a luxury I don't know. Even the kids started to play up: the eldest one was becoming really cheeky, the middle one was moaning all the time and the baby kept writing on the walls. When I put them to bed, it would be gone ten at night before they had gone to sleep, that was after they had created havoc and I had been up there half a dozen times. It seems like I was always shouting and hollering. Well, that was six months ago now and the boys have finally settled down. They are still naughty but not half as bad as

they were, at least they go to sleep now when they go to bed. My neighbour had a party which she invited me to, so I went and met some people – I met my eldest son's friend's mother and I met people at my middle son's playschool. I have now put my youngest son's name down for nursery, so I can go out to work. I have also learned how to mend a plug, fix a fuse and can do some painting. I still get creases in the wallpaper but never mind. When the warm weather comes we will be able to go out for the day without having to rush back to get the dinner and I don't have any shirts to wash and iron, no dirty socks, we can eat what we want and when we want to, no one moaning at me. Life is not easy being a single-parent family, but it is far better than worrying what mood he is going to be in or what he is up to now, and above all I have peace of mind which is far more important than anything else as far as I am concerned.'

Society assumes that everyone lives in couples. Even though there are approximately one million single parents in this country, it is still considered 'better' to be part of a couple rearing children. A woman on her own may face prejudices in terms of housing and treatment by social security, and other people may treat you with suspicion. You may be seen to have 'failed' because you have not maintained a relationship and have lost your partner. Such attitudes can make you feel isolated and lonely. If you can, try to keep in touch with other single parents who will understand and be sympathetic to your problems.

MEETING PEOPLE

Meeting people is not easy, especially if you have not had the opportunity for quite some time. There are national organizations which cater specifically for single parents (both men and women). Gingerbread is a membership organization which has local groups which meet on a social basis. It puts out a regular bulletin and provides a lot of useful and well-written information sheets on all sorts of different topics. The National Council for One Parent Families is a national organization campaigning around the needs of single parents. It will give information by letter and over the phone to single parents and has two offices in London. There are various self-help groups for single parents which arrange social events, outings, etc., and you can ask at your local library, health centre or doctor's surgery whether one exists in your area. There are many so-called singles' clubs, usually in large towns or cities, but these often have dubious reputations and purposes. All clubs, social groups and associations are hard to approach and often seem intimidating, but if you can get someone to go along with you, it will be less daunting. If you can't go with someone, then contact someone in the group first – the secretary perhaps – so that you know someone when you first arrive. You can always get to know people by getting involved in local actitities: tenants' groups, community centre, parent–teacher associations. If there is a Women's Aid group near you, you could join the support group and become involved in running a refuge or campaigning to get one. There may be a women's group which meets or a women's centre where a number of groups may meet regularly. You may decide to join evening classes which may be run by either the local authority or the Workers' Education Authority and cover various topics such as pottery and Spanish. You may just get to know your neighbours by meeting them on the landing or over the garden fence. What you need to do is build up confidence to approach people. You may be living next door to another single parent!

DAY CARE

The care of children during the day is most often seen as the responsibility of the mother, but provision of day care for children by someone or some organization is very important to single parents, particularly if they have jobs. Day care is roughly divided into two types: firstly, provision for under-fives of full day care in nurseries or at a child-minder; secondly, school-aged children need after-school care and holiday care, and possibly someone to take them to school if you work early in the morning.

Day care of this kind is very difficult to find unless you are prepared to pay for it, which, with more than one child, could add up to quite a large sum. Single parents, who mostly have very low incomes, are particularly hard hit by this problem, when it is often they who are most in need. However, it is possible to get free day care for your children provided by social services. Nurseries which are run by social services and are free, or charge a nominal fee, are very over-subscribed and it can be very hard to get a place for your child, though this can vary depending on the area in which you live. You may have to join a waiting-list for over a year before there is space. If you are a single parent, you may well get some priority for nursery places. If you are working, you will have to stress your need for a place, but you should get some help from social services if you say you are about to start a full-time job, even if it is only the name of a registered child-minder. If you do not work and do not want to work, you may still need some time during the day when your children can be looked after. There are many nurseries which provide only part-time care for a few hours a day, which are easier to get into. There are also places where you can go with your children where they can meet other children and you can meet other parents. For information about whether all these different schemes exist in your area, contact social services, the local library, local schools or community centres.

DAY NURSERIES

These may provide full-time or part-time care for your child. Even if they are open all day, they may only take your child, for example, from 9 a.m. to 12 noon. You can leave your children there and collect them later. They may be run by social services, in which case they are free, or they may charge a small amount. Full-time is usually from 8 a.m. to 6 p.m. to allow parents to work full time.

There may be a privately run nursery in your area, but these tend to be quite expensive: a cheaper one would be about £14 per week per child. They may be registered with social services, but this is no guarantee of good care. It is essential to visit the nursery before accepting a place.

SELF-HELP NURSERIES

These are usually run by groups of parents themselves on a rota basis. They may rent or have been given premises and possibly some funding to provide equipment. They have to charge a small fee, but often only if you can afford it. If you use the nursery, you could also be involved in the running of it. The large ones will be dependent upon funding of some sort, other than fees, so may be at risk of being closed at any time.

CHARITY NURSERIES

There are a few nurseries run by charitable organizations who fund-raise to keep going. They are very few and far between, have long waiting-lists and charge low fees.

NURSERY SCHOOLS

Some primary schools have a nursery school attached for the under-fives who are coming up to school age. They do not accept babies or toddlers. There is no charge for this and it allows the child to get used to school. There are, again, very long waiting-lists for places, but it is always worth finding out which schools have nursery departments and ringing them direct to put your case.

CHILD-MINDING

If you can't find a free nursery place, or you prefer your children to be in a closer environment, you can take them to a child-minder. Child-minders are mostly women who look after other people's children during the day, often as well as their own. You may see child-minders advertised locally in shop windows, or you may know of one through friends or relatives. Social services will recommend registered child-minders. To be registered, the child-minder has to fulfil certain conditions of safety and have suitable premises. They are not permitted to take more than a certain number of children, and then only children of certain ages. It is preferable, if you are being recommended to a child-minder, to check that they are registered. Payment does not vary greatly, but it is arranged between you and the child-minder; the average charge is about £10–15 per week per child, depending on the hours. Similarly, you will have to arrange between you how the children are to be collected, and so on. Some single parents employ child-minders only for the hours between school ending and when they finish work; some use them only for two to three days a week. If you go to social services, you should tell them what arrangements you would like and they can put you in touch with a child-minder who would be suitable.

Some women feel very uneasy about leaving their children with child-minders, and it is very hard to leave them at first. However, you should soon get to know the child-minder, and then you will feel much more confident about leaving your children with her. There can be no guarantee that the child-minder will get on with the children, but in most cases it works very well; the children learn to relate to another adult and will become fond of their minder.

PLAYGROUPS

There may be a playgroup in your area organized by a voluntary group, which is available to under-fives either every day or once a week. These are usually only for a few hours a day, but this is still enough to allow the children to get out. If there is a local community or youth centre or a family centre, you may find that they run a play group. Get in touch with all these places to ask.

PLAY CENTRES

These are attached to schools but run independently from the school. They are usually only for children from the school. They are organized mainly for the children of working parents who cannot collect their children until five or six o'clock. If your children attend a school where there is a play centre, you will still have to ask if they can be accepted. The play centre may only accept children of five upwards, which is a problem if your child starts school at four, or they may already be full up when your child starts. Play centres are for children aged five to eleven years old.

For older children, of eleven to sixteen, 'after-hours' clubs may be attached to the school.

BABYSITTING

A babysitter who comes to your home to look after the children can be anyone, as long as they are over fourteen years of age. This is a very piecemeal form of child-care, usually in the evenings. You can advertise for a sitter, but there is no guarantee that she will be reliable. Most often she will be a young girl who will charge at least £1 per hour, and it becomes very expensive if you want to go out a lot.

THINGS TO DO WITH YOUR CHILDREN

The local library, schools or community centres will probably have information on what clubs and groups exist in your area for children.

ONE O'CLOCK CLUBS

These are places where you can take your children for a couple of hours in the middle of the day. Often they are in parks, have toys for the children to play with, and may provide tea and biscuits. You are expected to stay with your children, although there may be staff present to keep an eye on things. These are good places to meet other women and children.

MOTHER AND TODDLER GROUPS

These are organized by community centres, on estates, or by the local authority, and are usually attached to a playgroup. Basically, they are places where women with small children can go and meet others.

TOY LIBRARIES

A toy library is a place where you can go with your children and borrow toys in the same way that you borrow books. There is usally space for children to play and somewhere for the adults to sit. Toy libraries are organized voluntarily and usually open about once a week; they particularly welcome handicapped children and have specially adapted toys for them. Find out from social services or contact the Toy Library Association to see if there is one in your area (see Appendix I). The Toy Library Association can also give you information about how to start one up yourself.

SELF-HELP GROUPS

There may be self-help groups in your area, that is, groups of women organizing their own shared child-care. For example, if you can find four or six other women with children of similar ages, and they each take turns to have all the children for one morning a week, you can organize to have at least four mornings a week free. Gingerbread has a leaflet on self-help day-care schemes, available from Gingerbread Association for One Parent Families, 35 Wellington Street, WC2, which tells you what information you will need to set up a formal scheme.

CLUBS AND ACTIVITIES FOR CHILDREN

There are hundreds of clubs, organizations and groups for children all over the country. There are organizations like Brownies, Guides, Scouts and Woodcraft Folk, which may have a local group in your area, or there may be clubs for young children which run locally (swimming clubs, for example).

YOUTH CLUBS

Once the children are old enough they can start going out on their own to youth clubs. These are run by either the local authority, the education authority or sometimes churches, and they organize activities for young people. Some have special nights for different sexes. They may be open every day or just once a week, depending on the area, and they may or may not have staff present.

LATCHKEY PROJECTS

These are run specifically for children after school, with activities arranged until early evening, when the parent will be back from work. They are different from after-hours clubs in that they are independent of the schools.

HOLIDAY PLAY SCHEMES

Many local authorities, schools, playgroups, clubs and voluntary groups organize playgroups in the holidays. These may be for just a week at Easter, but in the summer they may last from four to six weeks. Play schemes consist of different activities every day, for example, visits to the park or to theatre groups. They vary in how they are organized, you may have to deliver and collect your children, and you may have to pay a small amount each day.

GETTING EXTRA MONEY

Women who have had children will find it particularly difficult to get full-time work, because their work record has been interrupted and because employers are not keen to employ women, let alone women who have been out of the job market for years.

Women, in general, are in low-status, low-paid jobs. A high-income job would probably mean greater responsibility and longer hours, which would be a problem for women with children, and the longer the hours, the more of your income you'll have to spend on child-care. A high-income job may mean more flexibility to allow you to fit your working hours round your children. If you want to work full-time, you have to be prepared for the physical exertion required to work and look after the children, and also possibly to cope with feelings of guilt about not giving your full attention to them. This is really only a product of the pressure society puts on women to remain at home with the children, and does not take into account the fact that the children may be developing quite adequately spending part of their time in someone else's care. The main problems come from unsympathetic employers who will not allow flexibility when it comes to women with children who may need time off when the children are sick, or to go to school functions. Women with children would find it much easier to cope with full-time work and bringing up children if their employers took into account the fact that they are single parents.

The Equal Opportunities Commission (EOC) have published a booklet called *Fresh Start* – a guide for women on how and where to train for a new job. It's aimed at women who are returning to work after bringing up their families. It gives advice on training courses, types of qualifications, grants and how to get them, career offices, and job centres.

The National Advisory Centre on Careers for Women have published a book called *Returners*. Again, it's about women returning to work after a long time. It tells you how you can put to good use the skills you have learned over the years spent looking after children. It tells you what courses you can apply for to brush up the skills you used to have. It's available from NACCW, Drayton House, 30 Gordon Street, London WC1, or ask your local library to order it for you – it costs only 30p.

If you decide to start work, you have to calculate whether you will be financially better off or not, taking into account tax, travelling expenses, child-care expenses, the possibility of getting FIS, etc. It's not just a financial decision, however: you may decide you want a job just for the stimulation or status, or to get out of the house, or for the work experience which will be useful in the future. It is up to you to decide whether you would be better off (see Chapter 4 for information on how benefits are affected).

PART-TIME WORK

Part-time work is what most women consider the ideal compromise, but it is now very hard to find except in very low-paid and menial jobs, and if you have children you will still have to rely upon the understanding of an often unsympathetic employer. The sort of part-time work you can get will depend on what skills and experience you have and on the state of the job market in these areas.

The EOC have published a booklet called *Job Sharing*. This describes how two people can apply for one full-time job, either on a week-on/week-off basis, or each working 2.5 days a week or 5.5 days a fortnight. Job sharing is encouraged by the government, but is not that popular with employers; it's always worth trying, however. For the booklet, write to EOC, Overseas House, Quay Street, Manchester.

Remember that you can still claim SB and work up to thirty hours a week, and if you work more than twenty-four hours a week, you may be eligible for FIS. Some women manage to get paid work without declaring it to social security, so their benefit is not affected; this is usually cleaning or waitressing which is done off the cards. This is understandable considering the level of benefit single parents get, but you have no protection or security as an employee, and may be charged with fraud by the social security office if you are caught. This could mean a heavy fine or even imprisonment.

CHILD-MINDING

Many women look after other people's children to supplement their income, but this is only recommended if you really like children. To become registered, you will have to fulfil certain conditions; you should inquire at social services as to what these are. You can advertise without being registered, but parents prefer to go to registered child-minders and you would probably have to charge less. If you are claiming supplementary benefit, one third of what you earn will be treated as income and the earnings-disregard rule will apply; the rest will be ignored.

LODGERS AND SUB-TENANTS

If you can find room in your home, you could advertise for a lodger. You can charge rent either inclusive or exclusive of heating, lighting, etc., and you can decide whether or not to provide extra services like meals, laundry, etc. Before doing this, you should investigate your position as a landlady and whether you are creating a tenancy such that if you have trouble with your tenants, you cannot just throw them out and there are procedures you have to abide by. If you want a tenant only for part of the year, you could advertise in a local college for students who would be there only during term-time. If you want company, you could advertise for another woman with a child, if you have space, and you could then share living expenses. If you are claiming supplementary and housing benefit, or just housing benefit, there are set rates of deductions that are made for lodgers and sub-tenants, depending on what you provide. You can find out what these are in the section on benefits.

FRUIT PICKING

In rural areas, this can be a good way to make some extra money in the summer. It is seasonal work and realistic only for women who live near a farm. It is very hard physical work, but the children may be able to join in and earn some money too. Some won't allow pickers of under seventeen years old. It's not a good idea to take very young children, as they cannot be watched all the time.

WORKING FROM HOME

Homeworkers, who are mostly women, are notoriously exploited by commercial companies. They are among the very lowest-paid group, often getting less than 25 pence an hour for tedious and exhausting work. There is no protection for homeworkers under employment law, they are mostly non-unionized and have no security of employment. The advantages of working from home are obvious; you can regulate your own hours and do not necessarily have to pay for child-care. However, if your children are very small, it will be very difficult to look after them and work at the same time. Before you take on this sort of work, consider whether it will be worth while for you.

If you already have skills and resources, you may be able to use these to work at home: for instance, if you have a typewriter, you could do typing at home. You could advertise in shops or in local colleges. If you have a sewing machine you could advertise as a dress-maker or you could knit for individuals or for shops. The problem with this type of work is that it is very time-consuming and children are likely to prove a major distraction, but if you have the skills they can be profitable.

FURTHER EDUCATION

You may decide that you want to go to college and get some qualifications, or enrol on a course to learn a new skill. This could lead to greater job opportunities if you are intending to look for a job, or you may decide on a particular course out of interest. There are many different courses and different types of colleges, and you can find out from your local library or job centre what is available in your area. Many colleges and further education centres have crèches for the children of students, so it is possible for single parents with children under school age to go to college.

The different types of course will include part-time studies, full-time courses at polytechnics, universities or further education colleges, vocational training (which would mean you would be qualified to do a particular job at the end of the course), and also government schemes, such as the TOPs courses. These provide specific training for a job, but do not guarantee a job at the end of the course. They are usually shorter than college courses and may be as little as three months. To find out about TOPs courses, you should go to the local job centre and they will tell you what courses are available and how to apply.

FINANCE

As a single parent you will not have to sign on as being available for work at the unemployment office, so you can apply to a college and attend while still claiming supplementary benefit. Alternatively, you can apply to the education authority for a grant for the period during which you will be at college. You can apply for a grant after you have been accepted by a college and they should tell you how to go about it. It is worth while applying for a grant, as it will be slightly more than you get on supplementary benefit. Find out from the local library or job centre what colleges there are in your area, and if you are interested in applying to any of them, you can contact them yourself to ask for details about courses and how you apply. Alternatively, you can get these details from the job centre.

HOLIDAYS

Single parents, more than most people, need a holiday, but on a low income or social security this is virtually impossible. There is an organization called the Holiday Care Service which has information about different types of holidays including those suitable for single-parent families. Write to the service telling them what sort of holiday you are looking for, and they can send you details of accommodation, transport and possible sources of financial help for a holiday that seems most appropriate. Write or telephone to: The Holiday Care Service, 2 Old Bank Chambers, Station Road, Horley, Surrey (Telephone: Horley 74535).

Local Gingerbread groups often organize low-cost group holidays, so it can be worth joining to meet other adults. Gingerbread also has a holiday register which enables single parents to swap or share each other's homes at little or no cost: for instance, you could swap a flat in London with a house in the country. Gingerbread also has a sharing scheme where you could be matched up with another single-parent family to share a holiday and costs. They have a savings scheme which means you pay something towards your booked holiday each week or month – but you have to finish paying for it before you go away.

EXAMPLES OF DIFFERENT HOLIDAYS

For you and the children: Gingerbread takes over a holiday camp for a week each year and you can book through Gingerbread Holidays, Lloyds Bank Chambers, Cambourne, Cornwall. For children only: you can send your child on a holiday with other children organized by Gingerbread in places such as Wales or Yorkshire. The price of this holiday in 1983 was £50 per week per child which includes rail travel from your nearest station and full board.

GRANTS

Some social services departments can refer families for a holiday, or they can send older children on a holiday to stay with another family, so that you get a rest. They will pay for travel and accommodation but expect you to keep yourself. You will have to present social services with a very good case before they will offer to pay for your holiday. Some charitable organizations give grants to pay for holidays: these include Gingerbread Holidays (apply to them direct); Children's Country Holiday Fund (apply to them through Gingerbread); and Family Holidays Association (apply through Gingerbread). It is worth applying to these organizations if you think you are in desperate need of a holiday. Include with your application letters of support from, for example, Women's Aid.

OUT-OF-SEASON HOLIDAYS

These are cheaper than peak-time holidays – it might mean you miss the good weather and the children miss a week of school – but you also miss the crowds.

YOUTH HOSTELLING

For the strong and tough and for older children. You can walk, cycle or drive from hostel to hostel where overnight accommodation and cooking facilities are available. Conditions are quite basic, but comfortable, and you are usually expected to do some chores before you leave. Some hostels have family dormitories where you and the children can all sleep in the same room. Otherwise, they have strict single-sex dormitories.

You pay a small annual fee to join the Association and children aged 5–16 are free. For a free leaflet write to: Hostelling with a Family, Trevelyan House, St Albans, Herts., with an s.a.e.

HOW TO GET THERE

The cheapest way of travelling is probably by coach, which is also the most uncomfortable when you have small children. If you have a BR family railcard, you can travel cheaply by train. You can share a card with another family if you are a single parent, and there is a minimum of one adult and one child who can travel at one time with second-class fares.

SCHOOL TRIPS

The school may organize holidays for the children at different times of the year and you may be able to get a grant to pay for your child. Find out from the Education Office if you are eligible for a grant.

9. IMMIGRATION AND CITIZENSHIP

If you are not a British citizen and you do not have a stamp in your passport giving you indefinite leave to remain in the United Kingdom, it is advisable to make sure that you know what rights you and your children have to live in Britain. It is best to clarify your situation as an immigrant before taking any legal action in relation to your marriage or relationship, before making claims for benefits or housing, and before getting medical treatment or using educational institutions in this country. When you go to any of these places, you might be asked to show your passport, which they may say is for identification. However, the information in your passport might be passed on to the Home Office if they think you do not have a right to stay here, and you could find that you are suddenly being asked to leave the country. The officials may also refuse your claims or make you pay for medical treatment, thinking that you do not have any right to them, even when, in fact, you do.

Immigration and citizenship are very complex areas of law on which few solicitors can advise properly, so it is best to get in touch with an organization which specializes in this area of law; there is a list of useful places in Appendix I. They will either advise you personally or tell you where to go for help. You will need to show your advisers your passport, so it is important that you keep it with you when you leave home. Solicitors can give you free advice and help with forms and letters that you have to send to the Home Office if your wages and savings are not too high for you to qualify for the green form legal aid scheme. Otherwise, there are law centres and some types of advice agency which can help you free of charge, irrespective of your income. We cannot tell you all that you need to know about immigration and citizenship law in this chapter, but we want to point out the types of problem that might arise and how you can try to avoid or resolve them. Your status as an immigrant to this country could be affected by a change in your circumstances such as leaving your partner. If the Home Office has not already given you the stamp in your passport which allows you to live in Britain, it may be difficult for you to get permission to stay, especially if your partner has only a limited right to live here. Women are seen as dependants of their husbands, which means that you may be expected to leave with him if he has to go for any reason, whether you are still living with him or not, unless you have permission to stay here in your own right. The Home Office may put pressure on you to return to the country you came from because your marriage has broken down, and your husband's family might do this too. However, they should not make you take the blame for what has happened. You should be able to get the right to remain here, if your husband or fiancé lives here permanently, and even if he does not, you might be given leave to stay on compassionate grounds. It is best to try to establish a right to stay as quickly as possible, before you take any legal action against your partner.

You could also have problems as a result of changes in nationality or immigration law, through which some people have lost rights to British citizenship or to enter and stay in Britain without even knowing about it. Legal rights in these areas have changed frequently, either by a new Act of Parliament being passed, or by the Home Office altering the rules, which it can do whenever government policy on immigration changes. Court decisions on the meaning of the laws have also tended to remove people's rights. By breaking the rules, even without knowing they had done anything wrong, some people have lost the right to stay in Britain.

IMMIGRATION AND NATIONALITY LAW

Since 1905, when the number of people allowed to come and live in Britain was first controlled by law, governments have passed a number of laws which increasingly restrict the categories of people entitled to live in Britain or to become British citizens. Immigration law states the conditions under which people can enter or stay in Britain. Nationality law defines which people have a right to British citizenship. The most important laws stating what rights you have, at the time of writing this book, are the Immigration Act 1971 and the British Nationality Act 1981. There are, in addition, the immigration rules, which say how immigration law should be put into practice, and are as powerful as law. Changes in nationality law do not necessarily affect your rights under immigration law, and the fact that you were a citizen of the United Kingdom and Colonies does not automatically mean you can live in Britain. The immigration Acts were introduced in order to stop many people who had United Kingdom passports coming here, although they allow people with ancestral connections special rights to come and live in the United Kingdom. This complex situation arose because people in British colonies were at one time given United Kingdom passports and encouraged to come to England. However, since the 1960s, it has been government policy to make it increasingly difficult for them to come and live here. Although some people in British colonies were allowed to keep their citizenship of the United Kingdom and Colonies when their countries became independent, this did not mean they could necessarily enter or stay in Britain, because of the restrictions in the immigration Acts. The situation was rationalized by the British Nationality Act which abolished citizenship of the UK and Colonies and replaced it with three new types of British citizenship. Many former United Kingdom citizens are now only entitled to a type of British citizenship which does not give them any right to live in Britain, although anyone who came here before the Act came into force in January 1983, and was given the right to live here permanently, does not lose this. For people coming to Britain after January 1983, the main factor that will determine whether they can enter or stay in the country will be their citizenship, unless they have previously been given the 'right of abode' under the Immigration Act, which means that they are free of immigration control.

YOUR RIGHT TO LIVE IN BRITAIN

The conditions under which you can stay and the length of time should be stamped in your passport. They will depend on your nationality, how and when you first got permission to come into the country, and may be affected by the situation in which your husband first came here too.

Some people are not subject to immigration control, which means that they can live here indefinitely and do whatever they want to, such as work and claim welfare benefits. You will be free of immigration control if you are a British citizen, and there are a number of ways in which people can become British citizens, which we describe in the section on citizenship. The Immigration Act classifies some people as 'patrial', which only applies to people who came to Britain before January 1983, and means that they have the right of abode in Britain and are not subject to immigration control. The other advantages of patriality or British citizenship are that you cannot be deported (which we explain later in this section) and you do not lose your immigration rights by leaving the country for more than two years.

You are patrial if you were a United Kingdom passport holder or you are a Commonwealth citizen and either you or one of your parents was born, adopted, registered or naturalized in Britain; if you are a Commonwealth citizen and you married a patrial United Kingdom citizen before 1 January 1983; or, thirdly, if you were a United Kingdom passport holder and you have at any time lived in Britain for five years, provided that by the end of that time you had no restrictions on what you can do here.

There are a number of other ways in which it is possible to get permission to live in Britain with no restrictions on your stay. Some people have been allowed into the country on a permanent basis under special schemes – Asians from Africa come under a voucher scheme. Refugees have a special status which allows them to live here. Citizens of Common Market countries can move freely between member countries to take work, and they can take their families with them. Anyone who works in Britain for four years with a permit will then be allowed to stay permanently. People who are allowed into this country as dependants of someone who lives here will be allowed to stay as long as that person does, so if you came as the wife of someone who is a British citizen or living here with indefinite leave to stay, you will also be given the right to live here permanently. When you come to Britain as the fiancée of someone who lives here, it is necessary to marry within three months of arriving, and you will not be given indefinite leave to remain here until the end of a probationary period of one year. Once you have been given permission to live here with no restrictions on the length of time you can stay and what you can do here, you are classified as 'settled'. However, if you are not patrial or a British citizen, you lose this status if you leave the country for more than two years. You can also be made to leave if the Home Office decides that you should no longer be allowed to stay, although this does not often happen, and the decision is usually made because of a criminal conviction.

You will be restricted in the amount of time you can stay and what you can do if you do not come to this country under one of the above schemes. For example, anyone who first comes as a visitor is expected to leave again after a certain period, and is not allowed to work. Students are supposed to leave when their courses finish, and must pay for their education, although they may be able to do some part-time work. If your husband was given only limited leave to live in Britain, you will be expected to leave when he does. It is generally very hard to get permission to stay here permanently if you were first admitted temporarily for a particular purpose (to study, for example), although by marriage to a man who has indefinite leave to stay you can get this right too.

There is a risk that you could lose the right to live in this country by leaving your husband before the end of the probationary year, or by not marrying your fiancé. If the Home Office has not already given you permission to live in Britain, they may be reluctant to do so once you separate from him. Many husbands report the fact that their wives have left them to the Home Office. However, if he is allowed to live here permanently, you should be able to stay in this country, provided that you do not take any legal proceedings against him until you have been here for at least a year and have a stamp in your passport giving you indefinite leave to remain in this country. It is harder for you to get permission to stay if he has only a restricted right to live here, or if he is ordered to leave the country before you get this permission.

If the authorities decide that you have no right to stay in this country, there are two ways in which you can be made to leave. You may be 'removed' if you are classified as an 'illegal entrant' because you or probably your husband deceived the authorities when you first came to this country, or if you got permission to stay by deception. You may also have to go if a deportation order is made against you, or maybe if your husband is deported.

A deportation order is made by the Home Secretary on the recommendation of immigration authorities or a law court. The reasons for it may be that a criminal offence has been committed; that you have stayed in the country for longer than permitted; or that the Home Secretary thinks your presence is 'not conducive to the public good'. The fact that you did not know your husband had done anything wrong, that you no longer live with him, or that the children have British passports, does not entitle you to stay. However, your own immigration status may be such that you cannot be deported.

There is no right to appeal against a decision to 'remove' you, but you can apply to the High Court to try to prevent this from being done, although this is not very likely to succeed. You can appeal against a deportation order if it is not made on the recommendation of the court, as long as it was not made on national security grounds. It is always advisable to have representation if you wish to appeal, and help from a legal adviser in dealing with the Home Office. The appeal usually goes first to an adjudicator. If it is turned down you can ask for permission to appeal to the immigration appeal tribunal, which must be done within fourteen days of the adjudicator's decision. You may also appeal to the adjudicator, whether you are being removed or deported, about the country that the Home Office has decided to send you to. Although the chance of winning an appeal is not very high, you could also be allowed to stay through the discretionary powers of the Home Secretary, When a deportation order has been made, he may agree to let you stay a few weeks longer in Britain, if you get your MP to ask for this, or he can give you the right to live here permanently.

If there is no legal right to an appeal, or if it fails, it is possible to appeal on compassionate grounds to the Home Secretary, who has wide powers to let people stay in this country. A number of women have fought against Home Office decisions to make them leave and won, either with just a letter or after a public campaign for their right to stay. So do not give up if the law seems to be against you. Make sure that lots of people know about your situation and look for help in putting pressure on the government to let you stay.

To get a campaign going, you can get together with others in the same situation or get help from workers in advice agencies and Women's Aid groups. There has been a lot of support for people who are being made to leave Britain, and several campaigns have been successful in this way. Help has come from churches, trade unions, political parties, local community organizations, councillors, MPs and members of the House of Lords. Through publicizing your situation in the media and by petitions, you can win a lot of public support. Here is an example.

Najat Chaffee is a young woman from North Africa who has been living in London since 1979. She and her British-born son, Mohassin, left home because of the violence of her husband. The Home Office refused Najat permission to stay in this country because she had separated from her husband and he had since been deported. She had no right to stay here despite the fact that her son was born here and she had started to make a new life for herself. If she had been deported, Najat would have faced further threats and violence and would have had no means of support. Najat explained what happened:

> 'I stayed with my husband here for nine months; after that I left because he beat me and there were problems over money. I went first to Chiswick and then to Brent Women's Aid. When I went to a solicitor about the problems with my husband, she told me I would have to leave and go back to my country. She said my marriage was not valid because my husband was already married.
>
> At the beginning of 1982 I heard from the solicitor that the Home Office said I would have to leave. When I heard I went to see Women's Aid to see what I could do. I thought of getting married to someone so I could stay here. Women's Aid and the Asian Women's group in Brent started to get people together to help me fight the Home Office and to raise money. We started to have meetings about the campaign and sometimes I went to other meetings to ask people to help me and to sign my petition. I was interviewed by the television and newspapers and the group held a picket of my appeal and a local march through Brent.
>
> I lost my appeal, but while I was waiting for the next stage, I suddenly heard that I was being allowed to stay. I was very happy and we had a party to celebrate. Now I am working and Mohassin is in a nursery and I am trying to save some money to go on holiday. I wanted to stay here because my baby was born here and I wanted to see a future here for him. I want to tell other women in my situation not to give up hope but to try and fight back.'

YOUR RIGHTS TO WELFARE BENEFITS, HOUSING, EDUCATION AND MEDICAL TREATMENT

The immigration rules say you are not allowed to 'have recourse to public funds' if you have no leave or just limited leave to stay in Britain. This term has not been properly explained by the Home Office, so it is hard to say which state benefits you are definitely not entitled to. However, the main problem caused by this prohibition is that the authorities may notify the Home Office when you make a claim, and this may result in a decision that you do not have any right to live in this country. As long as you do not risk being told to leave the country, it is generally worth trying to claim what you need, and you do not have to show your passport as proof of identity, unless they need to check your status as an immigrant in order to decide whether you are entitled to make the claim. The DHSS can ask to see your passport as proof of your right to be here before giving you supplementary benefit or other welfare benefits, and your right to claim housing benefit is also likely to be dependent on your receiving indefinite leave to stay. As an overseas visitor, you are supposed to be charged for medical treatment if you have been here for less than a year. It may be worth while arguing that they should let you have a council house regardless of the length of time you might stay here, because there is no legal reason why you should not be entitled to it. If the local authority do refuse to house you because you are not allowed to live permanently in Britain, or if they say you made yourself homeless, by leaving your home in the country you came from, you will need help in persuading them to house you. Schools and nurseries may ask to see your children's passports before they will enrol them, but you are entitled to send your children to a state school if you are staying here for six months or more. Some people, even though they may have the right to live here, find they are discriminated against when they try to make use of the services provided by the state. Because not everyone who comes to this country is allowed to claim welfare benefits or free medicine, if you are black or have a pronounced accent, you may be subject to checks on your eligibility before being given what you are entitled to.

BRITISH CITIZENSHIP

Before January 1983, when the British Nationality Act 1981 came into force, many people had British passports as citizens of the United Kingdom and Colonies, although they did not all have the same rights to live in Britain. This Act created three new types of British citizenship. It states which category of citizenship anyone who used to be a United Kingdom citizen is entitled to, and under what conditions people can register or naturalize in order to take on British citizenship. If you automatically qualify for British citizenship, you can simply apply for a British passport. Anyone who was born in Britain before January 1983, or who is born after that date to a parent who is settled in Britain or a British citizen can do this. Adoption by a British citizen also gives this right. British citizens and people in Crown or other types of service abroad, whose children are born outside the UK, can claim British passports for them. People who had registered or naturalized in order to take on UK citizenship and patrial citizens of the UK and Colonies became full British citizens when the Nationality Act came into force.

Citizens of the United Kingdom and Colonies who did not have an automatic right to become British citizens in January 1983 took on one of the other types of British citizenship. People living in British colonies became British Dependent Territories citizens, and those living in ex-colonies, who kept British citizenship when that country became independent, became British Overseas citizens. People who took on these two categories of citizenship, or who are British protected persons or British subjects, do not have any right to live in Britain. However, anyone who is able to enter and stay here for five years can register as a British citizen once they have been given indefinite leave to stay. Many people living in Britain came from colonies as citizens of the UK and Colonies before the countries became independent. At independence, they generally became citizens of that ex-colony, although they might not have realized that this had happened. They did not lose the right to live here when they lost the UK citizenship, but it is now necessary to apply for registration or naturalization in order to become a British citizen. Just a few colonies negotiated independence agreements which entitled people from that country who were settled in Britain to take on British citizenship as well as their new citizenship, for instance, Antigua, Belize and probably others becoming independent after 1983. However, it will only be possible to have dual nationality if the other country allows it.

REGISTRATION

Registration is the method by which anyone who has an automatic right to British citizenship can become a citizen. It is very simple – you complete the paperwork and pay a fee. Registration is possible for children born in Britain after 1983 with a parent who obtains British citizenship or indefinite leave to remain in the United Kingdom after the birth of the child, and children born outside Britain to a parent who is a British citizen by descent, with a residential connection with the UK. Children who came from independent Commonwealth countries and were living in Britain in January 1983 are entitled to register for five years after they reach the age of eighteen, provided they continue to live in Britain. If you were married before January 1983 to a man who is a British citizen, you have until 1988 to register, provided that you are still married. Being separated but not divorced does not end this entitlement, but if you are widowed or divorced it is necessary to apply for discretionary registration, which can be refused. After that date there will be no automatic right to British citizenship as a result of marriage, although it will be possible to apply for citizenship through naturalization. If you came to Britain from an independent Commonwealth country before 1973, and you have been living here ever since, it is possible to register as British until the end of 1987. British Dependent Territories citizens, British Overseas citizens, British protected persons and British subjects can register after living in Britain for five years, if the final year is free of restrictions. Other people who wish to become British citizens must apply for naturalization.

NATURALIZATION

Naturalization is the way in which people who have a discretionary right to British citizenship can become citizens. It is more expensive and you could be refused, especially if you have problems with the police or financial problems. All applicants for naturalization must have been free of immigration restrictions for the past year and must have been living in Britain for a number of years. You can apply on the basis of being married to a British citizen in which case you need to live here for three years. Anyone who has had an unrestricted right to stay in Britain for five years, or who has lived here on a work permit and been given settled status, can apply for naturalization. Proof of good character is required, which may involve checks on your political activities and investigation to find out whether you have a police record. You must also speak English. It is not possible to appeal if you are refused, and applicants may be told to wait for two years before applying again.

Once you have become a British citizen you have the right to live in Britain with no restrictions. It is then possible to go away for long periods and be sure of the right to return. You will be able to live and work in Common Market countries, and in some forms of Crown or foreign service. The main advantage that it gives is the security that you will not lose the right to live here, claim welfare benefits, vote, and pass on your citizenship to your children.

YOUR CHILDREN'S RIGHTS TO CITIZENSHIP

Children who were born in Britain before January 1983 automatically become British and there is no need to pay for registration. Since that date, children born in Britain whose parents are not British citizens do not have any automatic right to British citizenship. The rights that they have depend on the nationality and immigration status of their parents – either you or their father if you are married, or just your status if you are not married. If you are a non-British parent, and you have an indefinite right to live in Britain, your children will be British citizens if they are born here. While you have a restricted right to live in Britain, on a student or visitor's visa, for example, you cannot register as British citizens your children who are born here. However, if you or possibly their father later become British citizens or settled here, any of your children who were born in Britain may be registered as British citizens. Children can also be registered in their own right after living in Britain for ten years, provided they have not been abroad for more than ninety days at a time, and the Home Secretary has wide powers to give any child British citizenship if he wishes to. It is possible that children who are not able to take on British citizenship could be stateless, if they cannot take the citizenship of either parent, so you should seek advice if you are not sure of your child's nationality.

Children who were not born in Britain can, while under the age of eighteen, come to join you, as long as you have permission to live here with no restrictions, or if you become a British citizen. However, if you are the only parent who is living in Britain, you have to show that you have sole responsibility for a child's upbringing before she or he will be allowed into the country.

10. SCOTLAND

The options that we have described in this book and the factors that may affect your decisions do not necessarily apply to your situation unless you live in England or Wales, because not all these courses of action are possible in Scotland and Northern Ireland. The court systems and many areas of law are different in those countries. In this book we are not able to do more than explain which rights you have there in common with England and Wales, and in which situations there are alternative possibilities. In each country there is a network of refuges which provide emergency shelter, advice and information. The central office of Scottish Women's Aid will be able to refer you to a refuge, answer your questions or suggest an appropriate agency to give you the help that you need.

MONEY

Throughout the British Isles you have the same entitlement to welfare benefits and housing benefit. If you are receiving supplementary benefit, you are automatically entitled to free legal aid, and if you are on a low income, you will have to pay only a small proportion of your legal costs, or nothing at all.

HOUSING

If you have to leave your home because of your partner's violent behaviour, you can go to the local council housing department and apply for accommodation under the provisions of the Housing (Homeless Persons) Act 1977. They have the same duty to ensure that you have somewhere to stay immediately and then a safe place to live in permanently that we have described in Chapters 2 and 3. The responses given by housing departments vary – some are very helpful, while others are not. However, you can generally expect to be rehoused if you are homeless as a result of domestic violence, provided that you are in priority need – that is, if you have dependent children, are pregnant, ill or elderly. If the local authority is reluctant to help, you can get assistance from the local Women's Aid group or other advice agencies. The Code of Guidance to the Housing (Homeless Persons) Act, published by the Scottish Development Department, is sympathetic to battered women and it is helpful to quote what it says to the local authority, although its directives are not legally enforceable. It makes it clear that you should not be treated as intentionally homeless and refused rehousing when you leave home because of violence, stating that 'it would clearly not be reasonable for you to remain'. This also applies where there has been 'severe emotional strain' rather than physical violence. The fact that violence has not yet occurred does not necessarily mean that it is not likely to occur, and the absence of proof should not be a reason for refusing the application. It says: 'It may be impossible to obtain evidence in the usual forms and in such cases the woman's fears may be considered as sufficient evidence.' If you have taken out a court order prohibiting your partner from being violent, but you feel that it is not effective, the Code states that this 'does not necessarily mean that it is safe for you to return home'. Your children do not have to be living with you at the time of the application in order for you to be accepted for rehousing, and, whenever possible, accommodation should be available for women without children. Where there are rent arrears which are not your responsibility the Code says that 'a spouse or cohabitee should not be held responsible for arrears accrued by the other partner as sole tenant', so you should not have to pay these off in order to be rehoused.

The other options which we described in Chapter 3 are also available in Scotland; you may apply for rehousing to a housing association, for example, or move to a new address by means of an exchange. The housing department might suggest that you apply under the Matrimonial

Homes (Family Protection) (Scotland) Act for court orders giving protection and the right to live in the matrimonial home, in order to try to avoid their responsibility to help, but the Scottish Development Department guidelines stress that you should not be expected to return home if you will not be safe there.

LEGAL PROTECTION

If you or your children are assaulted, threatened or harassed by your partner, there are a number of ways in which you can use the law to help you.

THE POLICE

You are entitled to police assistance if you are being assaulted and, if there is evidence of the assault, the man may be charged by the police and prosecuted. However, the police are not always helpful when you call them out and, even if he is taken to court, this may not be very effective in giving you protection. He may just be warned or fined, and there is nothing to prevent him from returning to your home and doing the same thing again.

INTERDICTS

You can apply under 'common law' in the Sheriff court for court orders, called interdicts, protecting you or your property. This might be done as part of wider proceedings, such as custody or separation, and would be particularly useful if you are being harassed or threatened by your ex-husband or a man you used to live with. If protection is needed urgently, you can get an interim interdict within a few days. This offers temporary protection until there can be a full hearing at which it will be decided whether there is sufficient evidence for the full order to be granted. Your solicitor should make sure that your partner receives a copy of the order, and a copy can be sent to your local police station. It is advisable for you to keep a copy of your interdict with you too. If your partner breaks it, he may be prosecuted by the police if he has committed a criminal offence, or your solicitor can raise an action for breach of interdict.

THE MATRIMONIAL HOMES (FAMILY PROTECTION) (SCOTLAND) ACT 1981

This is intended to give you a choice about whether or not to leave home if your partner is violent. You can be given an 'occupancy right', which is the right to live in the home even if you are not the owner or tenant, and the court has the power to exclude your partner from it, order a transfer of tenancy and make orders giving you more legal protection than is given by an ordinary interdict. It is the Scottish equivalent to the Domestic Violence and Matrimonial Proceedings Act and the Matrimonial Homes Act, which can be used only in England and Wales. You may use the provisions of this Act whether or not you are married to your partner, although you will be treated differently if you are cohabiting. When making an order, the court will take into consideration the conduct of each partner, the needs of any children and any other relevant factors, such as the particular needs of each partner. The court may make interim orders if it is necessary to respond quickly in order to protect your right to occupy the home or your possessions, but it is hard to satisfy the court that this should be done. The full court orders last until the marriage ends or your husband gives up his entitlement to the home, or until they are varied or recalled by the court. For cohabitees, the right to occupy the home is granted for an initial period of three months, which can be extended for further periods of up to six months. Other orders last as long as you have the right to live in the home, unless they are varied or recalled by the court. When the court orders have been granted, it is advisable to keep copies of them with you in case they are broken.

Your Right to the Home and Possessions

If you are married, you have a right to live in the matrimonial home whether it is owned or rented, in your name or your husband's. This is called an 'occupancy right'. You can enforce this right by making an application under the Matrimonial Homes (Family Protection) (Scotland) Act for an order declaring your occupancy right, unless you have signed a form renouncing this right. If you are not married, you do not have an automatic right to live in the home, but you can apply for an order giving you occupancy rights on the basis of factors such as the length of the relationship and the existence of any children. When the court grants an order declaring your occupancy rights, it can make other orders which enable you to enforce your right to live in the home, and you can be granted the possession or use in the matrimonial home of any furniture or plenishings. The court can also make an order restricting your partner's occupancy right.

Exclusion Orders

If you are married and you suffer conduct or threatened conduct from your husband which 'is or would be injurious to the physical or mental health of yourself or your children', you can be granted an exclusion order, even if he is the sole owner or tenant. In deciding whether to make these orders, the court considers whether his conduct offers a threat of immediate and real danger from which you need protection. If you are cohabiting and the home is in his name, you can be granted an exclusion order only if you are first given occupancy rights. When it is in your name or joint names, you can simply apply for an exclusion order because you have a right to live in the home through the tenancy.

You can also apply for interdicts prohibiting him from entering the home or removing the furniture or plenishings without your consent, and he can be prevented by an interdict from entering or remaining in a specified area near by. If you cannot gain entry to the home, the court can order him to let you in.

Protection

Whether you are married or cohabiting, you can apply for an interdict prohibiting your partner from assaulting, threatening or harassing you or the children. The same goes for women who are not using the Matrimonial Homes Act. Any interdict which is granted together with an exclusion order must have 'the power of arrest' attached if you apply for it. In other cases the court must grant the power of arrest, unless the man can convince the court that it is unnecessary. It means that your partner may be arrested if a police officer has reasonable cause to suspect that he has broken an interdict. The power of arrest is effective only after copies of the interdicts have been served on your partner and lodged with the chief constable of the area where you live. It is also best to get your lawyer to notify the local police station. Once your partner has been arrested, the police can release him only if they are satisfied that he will not be violent, and if he is not released, he must appear in court as soon as possible. If he is not arrested, your solicitor can take action for breach of interdict.

Transfer of Tenancy

You can apply to the court for the tenancy to be transferred to your name at any time during the marriage or when your decree of divorce is granted. If you are cohabiting, the court can transfer it only if you have occupancy rights. Your landlord will be informed of the application, but it is not possible for the transfer to be vetoed. You will not be liable for any of your partner's rent arrears when you take over the tenancy, although you both remain responsible if you were joint tenants. If the tenancy has been transferred and you wish to exclude your husband from the home while you are still married, it is necessary to apply for an exclusion order in addition to the tenancy transfer.

Problems That May Arise Using This Act

It can be effective only if the courts are willing to override male property rights and the police are prepared to intervene in cases of domestic violence. Although you may be able to get interdicts with the power of arrest attached, the police may refuse to arrest your partner if you are unable to convince them that he has broken the interdict, and they can also release him without taking him to court. The provisions of the Act may not, therefore, give you adequate protection if your partner persistently harasses or assaults you, in which case you can be sure of being safe only by having him locked up or by moving to a place where he cannot find you.

CRIMINAL INJURIES COMPENSATION

If your partner injures or assaults you or your children, you may be entitled to criminal injuries compensation. You must report any injuries to the police and cooperate with their investigations, and you cannot get compensation unless you stop living with him after the incident, unless the victim was a child. You can get an application form, and find out about the conditions under which you can get compensation, from an advice agency.

PERMANENT SEPARATION

When you want to end your marriage, you may take out divorce or separation proceedings, but you do not have to take any legal action. The legal ground for divorce and the ways in which you show that you should be divorced are the same as under English law, which we described in

Chapter 6. In Scotland, however, there is no minimum period for which you must be married before you may apply for a divorce based on unreasonable behaviour or adultery. If no decisions have to be made regarding children, money or property, and the divorce is by consent, you can do it yourself by filling out the necessary forms, if you are doing it on the basis of separation for two or five years. The forms are available from Citizens Advice Bureaux and other advice agencies. In all other cases it will be necessary to have a lawyer and the case will be heard by the local Sheriff court or the Court of Session. Legal aid may be available to pay your legal costs if you have a low income and no valuable property. If you have not come to an agreement with your husband, the court makes the decisions about custody, access and maintenance, in the same way as under English law. Scottish divorce courts do not have the power to order the transfer of ownership if you and your husband have bought or are buying the home. However, you may be able to come to an agreement that it should be sold or that one of you should buy out the share of the other. Otherwise, the court can order the payment of a lump sum from one partner to the other to compensate for the loss of any contribution made to the home.

CHILDREN

You and your husband have equal parental rights over the children until one of you obtains a formal award of custody in court. An application for custody can be made in the Court of Session as part of divorce proceedings, in the local Sheriff court as part of separation proceedings, or independently as an action for custody and/or interdict. You can apply in either of these courts while the proceedings are under way for interim custody and/or an interdict to prevent the children from being snatched. In Scotland, whoever has the child is considered to have custody until the court decides otherwise. It is advisable, therefore, to take the children with you when you leave home, or collect them as soon as possible afterwards, because your partner is more likely to be granted custody if he has been looking after them. If you are granted interim custody or full custody, he is likely to be granted access. We went into the questions of custody and access in more detail in Chapters 6 and 7.

11. NORTHERN IRELAND

The situation for women seeking to end a violent relationship is different in Northern Ireland from that in the rest of the United Kingdom. The legislation is different in relation to domestic violence, divorce, children, separation and housing, so much of the information in this book is not applicable to women living in Northern Ireland. If you live in Northern Ireland you will need to get in touch with Northern Ireland Women's Aid Federation, who will be able to put you in touch with a refuge and give advice on what you can do about your situation (you can find their telephone number in Appendix I). There are only a few refuges in Northern Ireland and you may not be able to move into one on your first attempt, but they will always be able to give advice and support.

The following chapter is a brief summary of what your statutory rights are in Northern Ireland, but for more detailed and expert advice contact NIWAF or any other advice agency or law centre. Although the legislation may be different, the considerations as to the effectiveness of legal action and the problems it causes will apply just as well to Ireland as to the rest of the United Kingdom. So, when considering whether to seek legal protection, for example, it is useful to consider how effective such action might be.

One of the major differences between the two countries is that in England there is legislation that allows cohabitees to take action against their partners, including getting a court order to remove him from the home. In Northern Ireland there are very few remedies for women who are not married and want to remain in the home without their partner. If you are not married you may, therefore, be forced to leave your home and seek alternative housing. The other major difference is that there is no Housing (Homeless Persons) Act in Northern Ireland. There are, however, provisions for women leaving home because of violence, and these are outlined below. The decision whether to stay in your home or to seek alternative permanent housing is one that you will have to make, taking into consideration the legal remedies available and the possibility of finding another home. There are legal steps you can take to get your home put into your name, or if you are a Northern Ireland Housing Executive (NIHE) tenant, the housing executive can transfer the tenancy at their discretion, provided you have custody of your children.

MONEY

The social security laws are the same in Northern Ireland as they are in the rest of the United Kingdom. Even the rates are the same, despite the fact that the cost of living is higher in Northern Ireland. The one difference is that in Northern Ireland there is the Payment for Debt Act, which allows social security to deduct a weekly sum from your benefit, without your consent, to pay rent, electricity or rates arrears.

HOUSING

Your options for finding alternative accommodation are much the same as those listed in Chapter 3: public housing from the NIHE, housing associations, buying, private rented accommodation and squatting. There is no statutory responsibility towards women forced to leave home because of violence, as there is no Housing (Homeless Persons) Act. Rehousing is up to the discretion of the local housing executive office, which for some women will be an advantage if their local office is sympathetic. However, you may equally find that you are refused housing by the housing executive, who can decide that you are not a priority case. In these circumstances, you have no legal redress: you cannot challenge their decision using the law, you can only get help from Women's Aid or advice centres to try to persuade the executive to change their decision. If you feel you have not been treated fairly you can make an application to the Commissioner for Complaints. The Commissioner will investigate to see if any maladministration has occurred, but he has no power to force the housing executive to change its decision.

The procedure for getting rehoused in Northern Ireland is relatively straightforward if you can get a legal separation. The major problems are for women who are not married and therefore have to rely upon a social worker's report, the length of time that you may have to wait in temporary accommodation before being offered a tenancy, and the standard of housing that is offered, given that Northern Ireland has some of the worst housing stock in Western Europe.

The provision of accommodation is the joint responsibility of the NIHE and the Social Services Boards, as there is no legislation which gives homeless people a statutory and enforceable right to accommodation. The social services boards have a discretionary power to provide temporary accommodation, and the NIHE has responsibility for rehousing on a permanent basis. Whatever sort of temporary accommodation you stay in should not affect your application to the NIHE for permanent housing, whether it be with friends or relatives, or in a refuge or a hostel.

TEMPORARY ACCOMMODATION

If you are forced to leave home because of your partner's violence, or if he has ejected you from the home, you will either go to friends, go to a refuge or another voluntary hostel, or approach social services for temporary accommodation. Social services have no statutory duty towards you, but they will usually try to refer you to a refuge or another hostel. They are very reluctant to pay for bed-and-breakfast hotels and therefore rely heavily on voluntary organizations to provide temporary hostel accommodation. It is possible to approach these hostels yourself, but they often prefer you to be referred by social services. Social services hostels are generally very unsuitable; they are often in bad condition and, as they are available to all homeless people, there is no mutual support from women who have had similar experiences which you would find in a refuge. Contact Women's Aid, if you can, to find a refuge space, or at least to make contact, so you can get support and advice during your stay in temporary accommodation.

While you are in temporary accommodation you will have to make decisions about what you want to do to sort out permanent accommodation. When you have made a definite decision and you want to move to another home, you should give up your previous tenancy as soon as possible, if it is in your name, to avoid building up rent arrears while you are in temporary accommodation. If the tenancy is not in your name, you will not be liable for any rent arrears. If you decide that you want to remain in the home, you will probably need to start some legal proceedings for protection and for a separation order. If you have an NIHE tenancy, once you have a legal separation and custody of your children, the district office will transfer the tenancy of your home to your name and normally rehouse your husband. It is possible to do this even if you have lived with your husband up until the time that your separation order is granted. Transfer of a private tenancy or owned property can be done only in the divorce courts.

FINDING A PERMANENT HOME

You will most probably rely on public housing to provide you with a new home, and this means making an application to the NIHE. When you make your application, the housing executive office will expect some proof that you cannot return to live with your partner. It will accept either a court order of legal separation or, if you are not married or cannot get this for any other reason, a social worker's report verifying your urgent need for housing. When you apply for housing, it takes approximately three weeks for your application to be processed, and you are then categorized by the housing executive according to your circumstances. You can apply to the housing executive regardless of what type of tenancy you held previously.

You may be considered for emergency rehousing if you have left home because of violence, but normally only if you have a legal separation order or a divorce or judicial separation. If you have none of these, the social services can make a report to support your application, in which case you may need evidence from solicitors, doctors or the police. The housing executive then decides whether it can provide emergency housing on the basis of the report. In practice, it takes longer to get a social worker's report than it does to get a legal separation in the Magistrates' court, and as a result married women usually get rehoused sooner than cohabitees. If you do not have children, you may still be regarded as a priority, but rehousing may take longer. When you have made your application, an officer will visit you wherever you are staying temporarily, and will ask you what your circumstances are and where you want to live. This may take about a month to arrange, and you will then have to wait for an offer of accommodation.

Generally, the housing executive office should accept you as a priority as soon as you get a legal separation order, so you should send a copy or the order, as soon as you get it, to the housing executive office.

RESIDENTIAL QUALIFICATIONS

When you apply in normal circumstances to the NIHE for housing, you have to have been living in Northern Ireland for seven years, or have been born there. This may not apply if you are being housed as a priority and therefore should not apply if you have left home because of violence.

Once the decision has been made to accept responsibility for offering permanent housing, your application is sent to the two areas of choice that you have specified, and you will then be made an offer of accommodation. The length of time you have to wait depends largely upon what area you want to move to: some are in more demand than others. For a popular area, you may have to wait over six months before getting an offer. You may not be given a completely free choice of where to live when you are rehoused as a priority. In certain circumstances, the NIHE can restrict areas where accommodation is offered; for example, when there are high rent arrears. The housing executive only has to make two reasonable offers, and if you refuse both of these, you will be put on to the general housing waiting-list, where there is little chance of being offered housing at all.

RENT ARREARS

If you had a joint tenancy or a tenancy in your name only, and have accumulated rent arrears, you may be asked to make a voluntary agreement with the housing executive to pay a certain amount each week when you apply for permanent housing. If you have rent arrears, you may be restricted to particular areas for rehousing, and your application may take longer to be given priority status. If you are claiming social security benefits, you may find that the housing executive is taking an amount from your money under the Payment for Debt Act.

It is possible to apply for a new tenancy from the housing executive even if you are still living with your husband, providing you have already been granted a legal separation order from the court, and you have custody of the children. If your husband refuses to move out of the house, you can still be awarded priority status and rehoused elsewhere.

USE OF EXCLUSION ORDERS

If you are married, you can get an exclusion order to remove your husband from the home, but the housing executive office will accept that getting such an order will not alter the tenancy rights of your husband, and they will not often insist that you take this type of legal action. The responsibility for getting your husband out of the house is not often left with you, and if you do get an exclusion order, the housing executive will not expect you to return home if you feel it is not safe. Cohabitees cannot get exclusion orders from the court, so unless your partner leaves voluntarily, you have no legal means of getting him out, and your only option is to give up the tenancy and apply for a new one. Once you have given up your tenancy, the housing executive may try to evict your partner from the home, but they very often just leave him there. If they have a responsibility to rehouse him, they may leave him, because there is a severe shortage of single-person accommodation.

PRIVATE RENTED

Similar conditions apply in Northern Ireland as in the rest of the United Kingdom regarding the private rented sector: it is very hard to come by, and particularly so if you have children.

HOUSING ASSOCIATIONS

You may either get referred to a housing association by social services or the housing executive office, or approach them yourself, but the amount of housing they have is quite small. Most housing associations have the same requirements and policy as the housing executive, so it is a very restricted option for women who are not accepted by the housing executive.

SQUATTING

If you decide to squat, there may be many problems, apart from the condition of the property, lack of security and other disadvantages which are mentioned in Chapter 3. You may not be able to get the electricity supply connected, and it could affect future applications to the housing executive for permanent housing.

LEGAL PROCEEDINGS

The possible legal proceedings that you can start in Northern Ireland are different from those in England, Scotland and Wales. There are laws you can use to get a divorce, custody of your children and maintenance from your husband, but the procedure for getting them is not the same as in the rest of the United Kingdom. There are laws which are intended to provide legal protection for women with violent husbands, but the same law does not cover cohabitees as well as married women. The problems of court orders, the unwillingness of the police to intervene, and women being faced with unsympathetic judges, are just as they are in the rest of the United Kingdom. You will have to consider, therefore, the effectiveness of taking legal action against your husband, when you make decisions about your future and that of your children.

You will certainly need to find a good solicitor with experience of matrimonial and domestic violence law. You may be entitled to legal aid, which can pay all or part of your legal costs, so go to a solicitor who takes legal aid cases. You can usually find one from the legal aid list which is available from local advice centres, CABs and libraries. For advice about your legal options, you can contact Women's Aid or a local advice or law centre. They will explain to you the difference between taking action to try to stay in the home, and what you can do if you decide that you want to leave home and move elsewhere.

The Domestic Proceedings (Northern Ireland) Order 1980 introduced provisions for married women to get personal protection orders and exclusion orders from the Magistrates' court. You can apply for either of these orders at the same time as applying for maintenance or legal separation, but you do not *have* to begin any matrimonial proceedings if you are applying for legal protection. If you are not married, you cannot use this law and you will have to rely upon other, rather limited, options.

PERSONAL PROTECTION ORDER

This orders your husband not to use violence or the threat of violence towards you or any of your children. To get such an order, you will have to prove that your husband has either threatened or committed violence against you or the children. In practice, the definition of violence is very physically oriented and it may be difficult to get a personal protection order, or an exclusion order, unless you can prove that there has been actual physical violence.

EXCLUSION ORDER

An exclusion order can order your husband to leave your home. It may say that he cannot come within a certain distance of where you are living, or it may specify a place, other than your home, where he is not permitted to go – a refuge, for example, or your parents' house. The court will order your husband to leave, forbid him to sell or damage the home or any of your possessions, and will forbid him to give up his tenancy. Although possibly not specified in the order, these conditions will still apply. An exclusion order is a temporary measure and can only last for a maximum period of six months, depending on what is specified by the judge. After six months you can apply for a renewal of the order.

INTERIM ORDERS

If you need to get a court order urgently, then it is possible to go to court the same day to get a temporary, or interim, order. These become effective from the time they are served on your husband and can last up to five weeks, during which time you can apply for a full order.

POWER OF ARREST

A power of arrest is attached to all relevant orders made in the Magistrates' court, but the power is discretionary and the police can choose not to arrest your husband if he disobeys the court order. Before they arrest him, the police have to be satisfied that you are in immediate danger from your husband. More often than not, the police will not arrest him. If they do, however, they have four options: to release him, or to release him on condition that he appears in court or reports to a police station, or to hold him until he appears in court within twenty-four hours. In most cases the police will merely release him unconditionally.

UNMARRIED WOMEN

If you are not married you cannot use the Domestic Proceedings Order to get legal protection from the court, and your options are therefore much more limited. In recent months, cohabitees have been able to get injunctions under common law to restrain a partner from using 'battery', which means intending to harm someone. This is similar to a personal protection order, and does not have the power to exclude your partner from the home. If you want to attempt to use this law, go to see a solicitor who is experienced in this type of situation.

You can try to get the police involved and try to get them to issue criminal proceedings for assault against your partner. If he has a conviction for breach of the peace, you can apply to the Magistrates' court to have him 'bound over', although this is not easy to do and does not mean that he is excluded from the home. Alternatively, if you are the tenant or owner of your home, you can sue your partner in the County court or High Court for trespass and damages. Once these proceedings have been started, you can apply to the court for an injunction to exclude him from your home. If you are not the sole tenant, it is extremely hard to force your partner to leave the home, and you will probably be forced to leave yourself and apply for rehousing from the NIHE.

LEGAL SEPARATION

The Domestic Proceedings (Northern Ireland) Order 1980 introduced the right for married women to apply to the Magistrates' court for a legal separation order. To make such an application you have to prove:

1. That your husband failed to make adequate financial provision for you.
2. That your husband failed to provide or make a proper contribution towards maintenance for the children.
3. That your husband committed adultery.
4. That your husband behaved in such a way as to make it unreasonable to expect you to live with him.

If you have already been separated from your husband and you have both agreed to live apart, you can still apply to the Magistrates' court for a separation order. You have to have been living apart by agreement, neither one having deserted the other, for a continuous period of at least three months, and either you or your husband should have been making payments of maintenance for the children. When the court makes the separation order, it can merely 'rubber stamp' the maintenance arrangements you have already made.

Once your solicitor has made the application to the court, you should

get a court hearing within six weeks to three months. The court can then make an order to decide:
a) that you no longer have to live with your husband;
b) who will have custody of the children;
c) what maintenance your husband has to pay you;
d) what maintenance your husband has to pay to the children (maintenance orders for children continue only until they are eighteen years old or while they are in full-time education, unless there are special circumstances justifying continued maintenance);
e) who is to pay the legal costs – but if you are entitled to legal aid you may not have to pay any costs.

RECONCILIATIONS

Before the court makes an order concerning maintenance, it has to consider whether there is a possibility of a reconciliation, and if there is, the court will adjourn the proceedings so that a reconciliation can be attempted. Meanwhile, the court can make interim, or temporary, orders concerning maintenance and custody. If there is any sort of delay the court is empowered to make interim orders.

A separation order, once it is made, will lapse if you are still living with your husband six months after the date of the order. It will continue to be valid if you return to live with your husband at any time, as long as it is not for a continuous period of longer than six months. You can, therefore, attempt a reconciliation for a shorter period, and the separation order, including maintenance and custody arrangements, will still apply.

MAINTENANCE

Husbands and wives are now treated equally in their obligations to maintain each other and any children, so it is possible for you to be ordered to pay maintenance to your husband – though very unlikely. The court can make an order for maintenance, provided that you last lived together in Northern Ireland, and you should make your application to the Magistrates' court in the area in which you or your husband live. Once the order for maintenance is made and if your husband does not pay, the court can issue an arrears summons. If he still refuses to pay, the court can order that his possessions be sold in order to pay the arrears. Alternatively, the court can commit him to prison, and imprisonment wipes out any arrears which have built up.

Supplementary Benefit

As in the rest of the United Kingdom, if you are claiming supplementary benefit, then this will be reduced by the amount of maintenance you receive. If your husband is unreliable about paying maintenance, he can be made to pay it direct to the DHSS, so that you can claim full supplementary benefit.

Different Types of Maintenance

The court can make four different types of maintenance order instructing your husband to pay

a) weekly, fortnightly or monthly payments to you;

b) a lump sum to you, for which your husband may have to provide some security to show that he can make the payment (you may be awarded a lump sum to cover the period between separating from your husband and making an application to the court. These lump-sum payments are not taxed as income, but will be deducted from supplementary benefit);

c) weekly, fortnightly or monthly payments for children;

d) a lump sum for the children.

Amount of Maintenance

The amount of maintenance you will get, as specified by the Magistrates' court, depends mostly on the income of your husband. If he is claiming social security, it is a good idea to get a maintenance order, even if it is only for a nominal sum, so that if he starts work, the order can be changed to a larger amount with a variation order. This is easier than making a fresh application. Your husband can also apply to have the amount decreased, if your income increases. Your income is taken into account when deciding the amount, but you will not be expected to support yourself and the children on your own. The general principle is that you should not have to endure a lower standard of living than your husband.

PROPERTY

The Magistrates' court has no powers to make any orders in connection with property. It can make an order to exclude your husband from the home – an exclusion order – but cannot transfer the tenancy or, if you own your home, transfer the ownership, to you. If you want to apply to the court to have your home in your name, you will have to apply to the County court or the High Court, in divorce or judicial separation proceedings.

CUSTODY

Custody will usually be awarded to you if the children are under eighteen years old, but the court will almost always grant reasonable access to your husband unless it decides that he is a bad influence on the children. It is possible for the court to grant actual custody to one partner and legal custody to the other. Legal custody means making decisions about the upbringing of the children, but not actually living with them. The court will ask for welfare reports to be prepared while considering the question of custody of the children, and can order that the children must not be taken out of Northern Ireland.

DIVORCE

If you want to apply for a divorce, you will have to prove that your marriage has broken down irretrievably. To do this you have to prove one or more of five facts:

1. Adultery.
2. Unreasonable behaviour such that you cannot be expected to live with your husband. This can be shown by various types of behaviour, including cruelty – both mental and physical – 'constructive desertion' – which means that you are forced to leave home because of your husband's behaviour – and behaviour resulting from unsoundness of mind.
3. Desertion by your husband. You have to show that your husband left home of his own choice and without your consent. It is possible to claim that your husband has deserted you, even though you live under the same roof, if all contact between you has ended. You must be separated in this way for two years before you can petition for divorce.
4. If you and your husband have agreed to live apart for at least two years and both consent to the divorce.
5. If you have been living apart from your husband for five years and one of you wants a divorce.

If you have been married for less than three years, you will be able to get a divorce only if you can prove that you have suffered 'exceptional hardship' or that your husband has been guilty of 'exceptional depravity'. In practice, it is very hard to prove either of these things, even if your husband has been extremely violent. The courts will often not accept violence as causing exceptional hardship, and as a result many women are not able to get divorced until the marriage has lasted three years. In this situation, it is better to apply for maintenance and a separation order from the Magistrates' court, and apply for a divorce later. Having already been granted a separation order does not prevent you from making an application for a divorce, neither do you have to have a separation order to enable you to petition for a divorce. If you do already have a separation order, the arrangements made in the Magistrates' court will not usually be altered during divorce proceedings, although it is possible for the County court or High Court to overrule previous orders. If you remarry following your divorce, you will have to inform the Magistrates' court of the fact. When the court hearing is over, you will be granted a decree nisi and six weeks later, provided that the court is satisfied with the arrangements that have been made regarding the children, you will be granted a decree absolute, which finalizes your divorce. In general it takes approximately nine months to go through the whole procedure.

Property

The County court or High Court can make an order concerning property when it deals with divorce or judicial separation. It can either transfer property into your name – for instance, if you want to stay in the home, the court can transfer a tenancy into your name or order that a home that you own should be transferred to your name only – or it can make a property settlement, which means you can benefit from the property but it remains in your husband's name: for example, the court might order that you should live in the matrimonial home, but it remains in your husband's name.

12. CONCLUSION

Women who seek help because their partner is violent are often told to change their behaviour – the way they look, the way they talk, the way they act – in order to 'solve' their problem. Social workers advise visits to the doctor and the doctor prescribes tranquillizers. Police officers who are called to the home rarely arrest a violent man, or offer any practical help; they may tell a woman to contact the social services or Women's Aid, but usually they wait until the 'argument' has cooled down, and then leave. It is not surprising, then, that women come to the conclusion that it is their fault that their partner is violent or abusive, that they provoke him in some way and that the solution to the problem lies in their hands.

However, it is the actions of men, whether they are physically, mentally or sexually abusive, that create the problem of domestic violence. A woman who is told to deal with her partner's violence by behaving differently, by adapting her behaviour to his, or by taking drugs, is simply being told in a roundabout way to put up with the violence. Certainly, it is clear that it is impossible to stop men from being violent just by making laws, and existing laws are inadequate in offering women protection and a means of escape. Male violence is deeply rooted in our society, and the only solution that can be offered to individual women caught in violent relationships is getting free. Thus, although it is not women who are to blame for the violence, it is they who are forced to uproot themselves and leave their homes as a result of it. Women will find this a lot easier when society in general and statutory agencies in particular become more sympathetic to their position and treat the problem more seriously. Social services, housing departments, doctors, police officers and judges should all be aware of how serious a problem domestic violence is and should be looking for ways of helping women to escape, rather than trivializing the problem and forcing women into attempting reconciliation. Equally, they should stop treating domestic violence as a private matter that can be dealt with only within the family and with which they should not interfere. Existing family power relations always work to sustain male power and therefore male violence. The threat posed by women leaving men and breaking up families is one that makes all men feel uncomfortable, and it is partly this which leads women to blame themselves and to try to revive the relationship.

The two major pieces of legislation intended to confront the problem of domestic violence – the Domestic Violence Act and the Housing (Homeless Persons) Act – have been shown to be quite insufficient to help women to escape domestic violence, and as a result many women are forced to return to, or remain in, violent relationships, instead of being helped to get out of them. This is because domestic violence injunctions have proved ineffective against a man who chooses to be violent, and because permanent rehousing is not offered to all women who apply for it after leaving home. If this legislation were made more effective, many more women would use it; at present women attempt to use it and are deterred when the injunction fails to keep the man away and is not enforced, or when they are refused safe rehousing. Further, statutory agencies such as the social services are often ignorant of the provisions of existing legislation, and give women wrong information – for instance, telling women that if there is no room for them at the local refuge, they must return home.

The spirit of these laws is reasonable, but adequate practical application is lacking. It would be easy to tighten up the domestic violence legislation by attaching powers of arrest to every injunction as a matter of course, and by forcing the police to act when an injunction is broken. It is impossible to prevent men from being violent, but this is one way in which the law could be seen to be more powerful. Many groups, including Women's Aid, have campaigned to make the Code of Guidance to the Housing (Homeless Persons) Act legally enforceable, so that the good intentions within the code could be put into practice and women could be offered a means of escape from violence, instead of falling through loopholes in the Act.

Both the Domestic Violence Act and the Housing (Homeless Persons) Act should be available as solutions to more women, including women who are mentally abused, women who suffer violence from someone other than a husband or boyfriend, and women who do not actually live with the man who is being violent. Existing laws do not always offer protection or escape to women if it is their children rather than they who are being sexually or physically assaulted by their partner: women may be told that they cannot apply for rehousing if they have not themselves been battered.

Having these two pieces of legislation means that they are often used as alternatives to one another. This should not be the way in which the legislation is used: the use of one resource should not deny women the right to use the other. For example, the use of the Domestic Violence Act to get legal protection should not mean, as it does at present, that women are then refused alternative housing. Local authority housing departments should not use injunctions as a solution to the housing problems of battered women and should certainly not force women to use this option when they don't want to.

There should also be more facilities for children when their parents split up. Their needs often become a secondary consideration when housing and legal proceedings are a major problem. There should be more widely available services to provide for supervised access, so that children can see their father if they want to, without endangering their mother or exposing her to further abuse from her ex-partner. If this were available, it would be possible to allow children more say in what happens regarding access arrangements. Solicitors and the courts must realize that access is a serious problem for battered women because of the high risk of being traced, so that the man can come back to cause more trouble.

The custody of the children can be the most difficult part of the divorce proceedings – men frequently contest the woman's application for full custody simply to cause trouble, even when they do not really want the children to live with them. The decision as to who has the children should not depend on who has the most suitable accommodation at the time; this often works against women who have been forced to leave home because of violence, and have gone to a refuge or temporary accommodation while they try to sort out permanent housing. Women have been denied custody on the grounds that they are living in a refuge, when the preferable solution would be to offer suitable alternative housing more quickly. Women should not be made to wait until legal proceedings such as custody, divorce and judicial separation have been finalized before getting permanent housing.

Given that women do have to spend time in temporary accommodation, there should be more resources available to increase facilities and standards of temporary accommodation, making more provision for women with children and also providing accommodation suited to the needs of women on their own. Refuges can offer this; but there is a need for much more funding for refuges – to cover the existing work of refuges, to increase facilities for children and for women who have left the refuge, and to enable more refuges to open; there is nothing like enough refuge space throughout the country. The recommendations of the Select Committee into Violence in the Family have not been fully implemented at all, and the demand for refuge space far exceeds the provision. Apart from refuges where women can go for help, and can stay if they want to, there should be many more places where women can go for help and advice, particularly in rural areas where there is a shortage of any kind of service.

If women are to feel confident about making the break from a relationship with a husband or boyfriend, they also have to feel confident about having a regular, secure and adequate income. At the moment, most women who live alone or with their children rely on social security, which is barely enough to bring up children on. The welfare benefits that women receive should be raised to a realistic level; while women are living with men they should not be forced into financial dependence on them, but should be able to claim benefits in their own right. It can be a cause of great hardship for a woman when the man she lives with has sole access to, and control over, their joint income, as this gives him the power to withhold it; it often happens, for instance, that while the man is given the money to pay for the rent, the woman is later held responsible for arrears when she takes charge of the tenancy.

Finally, there should be far more provision for, and understanding of, the problems of single parents. There is an urgent need for much more in the way of free day-care facilities, and provision of crèches in public places like supermarkets, launderettes, etc. There are thousands of single parents now living in the United Kingdom; employers should be more aware of their problems and more willing to offer jobs to women with children, or to offer job-shares.

With existing legislation, and with the existing attitudes of police officers, the courts, social workers and judges, we cannot solve the problem of domestic violence by trying to change the way in which individual violent men behave. Nor can women hope for any solutions from therapy, whether it is family therapy or therapy for their partners which is offered. Indeed, all too often medical and therapeutic agencies suggest therapy only for the women concerned. Agencies must start to treat domestic violence as a serious problem. Legislative agencies must start to envisage long-term solutions which enforce the rights of women within the family: the right of women to have control over their bodies and reproduction; and to separate, sufficient incomes; and to equal employment opportunities. Where these rights are violated, they must start to find solutions which will provide women with realistic opportunities to escape violence and abuse and to be rehoused in safe, decent, permanent accommodation, where they can be free from violence, the threat of violence, and the fear of discovery.

APPENDIX I
Useful Addresses

The following is a list of organizations which can give you information and/or advice on the topics covered in this book. Some are specifically mentioned in the text but there are many others which are not, including many independent advice centres. You can find out from social services whether there is one in your area.

Women's Aid Federation (England), 52/54 Featherstone St, London EC1 (01–837 9316) will give advice on the phone or put you in touch with a local Women's Aid group where you can get advice, support and refuge if you need it. There is a twenty-four-hour answering service.

Asian Women's Aid can be contacted through the federation.

There are also federations in Wales, Scotland and Northern Ireland:

Welsh Women's Aid, Incentive House, Adam St, Cardiff. 0222–388291.
Scottish Women's Aid, 11 St Colme St, Edinburgh. 031–2258011.
Northern Ireland Women's Aid, 143a University St, Belfast 7. 0232–249358.

The WAFE has several regional offices which can put you in contact with local groups , and an office in the north which deals with publications.

Bristol:	Regional office and women's centre Mon.–Fri. 10 a.m.–4 p.m. 24-hour answering service.	0272–22760
Doncaster:	Advice Centre Mon.–Tues. 9 a.m.–5 p.m. Wed.–Fri. 9 a.m.–9 p.m.	0302–857588
London:	Regional office Mon.–Fri. 10 a.m.–5 p.m. 24-hour answering service.	01–837 3762
Manchester:	Regional office and centre Mon.–Fri. 10 a.m.–4 p.m. 24-hour answering service.	061–2366540
Newcastle upon Tyne:	Women's centre and office Mon.–Fri. 10 a.m.–10 p.m. Sat.–Sun. 6.30 p.m.–10 p.m.	0632–614511
Nottingham:	Women's centre and Women's Aid centre Mon.–Fri. 10 a.m.–3 p.m.	0602–46490

These numbers and times may change, but they can be found through the telephone exchange.

National Association of Citizen's Advice Bureaux, 110 Drury Lane, London WC2 (01–836 9231) will tell you where your nearest CAB is.

Law Centres Federation 164 North Gower St, London NW1 (01–387 8570 and 01–278 4575) will tell you if you have a law centre in your area.

Legal Action Group, 23a Highgate Road, London NW5 (01–485 1189) will tell you where you can get free legal advice.

HOUSING

Shelter National Housing Aid Trust, 157 Waterloo Road, London SE1 (01–683 9377) have an office in London and will refer you to the nearest housing aid centre for advice.

SHAC, 189a Old Brompton Road, London SW5 (01–373 7276) will give advice over the phone for women in London.

Housing Advice Switchboard, 47 Charing Cross Road, London WC2 (01–434 2522) will give advice over the phone to women without children.

MONEY

Child Poverty Action Group, 1 Macklin St, London WC2 (01–405 5942) will give advice over the phone mainly for urgent inquiries. Ring between 2 and 5.30 p.m. on weekdays.

Disability Alliance, 25 Denmark St, London WC2 (01–240 0806).

LAW

Rights of Women, 52/54 Featherstone St, London EC1 (01–278 6349) have advice sessions for women about the law.

CHILDREN

Children's Legal Centre, 2 Malden Road, London NW5 (01–359 9392) will give legal advice for and about children: 2–5 p.m. on weekdays.

Family Rights Group, 6–9 Manor Gardens, London N7 (01–272 4231) will give advice on care cases.

Incest Survivors Group, c/o AWP, Hungerford House, Victoria Embankment, London WC2, will offer support to women and is also involved in campaigning.

Toy Library Association, Seabrook House, Wyllyotts Manor, Darkes Lane, Potters Bar, Herts. (Potters Bar 44571).

LIVING AS A SINGLE PARENT

Gingerbread, 35 Wellington St, London WC2 (01–240 0953).

National Council for One Parent Families, 255 Kentish Town Road, London NW5 (01–267 1361).

IMMIGRATION

Joint Council for the Welfare of Immigrants, 44 Theobalds Road, London WC1 (01–405 5527) will give advice over the phone on immigration and nationality, but you must have an appointment in order to see anyone.

The Home Office, Lunar House, 40 Wellesley Road, Croydon, Surrey.

British Refugee Council, Bondway House, Bondway, London SW8 (01–582 6922).

SCOTLAND

Scottish CAB, 82 Nicolson St, Edinburgh.
Scottish SNHAT, 6 Castle St, Edinburgh.

NORTHERN IRELAND

Belfast Law Centre, 62–66 Bedford St, Belfast (246984).

APPENDIX II
The Matrimonial and Family Proceedings Bill

During 1984 it is likely that the Matrimonial and Family Proceedings Bill will become law and therefore make significant changes to divorce law in England and Wales. Your solicitor should know the details of these changes and act for you accordingly, but it is useful to know the basic points of the Bill so that you can instruct your solicitor. The Bill is primarily concerned with the financial consequences of divorce and maintenance arrangements between spouses, and does not affect women who are not married even if they are seeking maintenance from the father of their children.

The first major provision of the Bill is to alter the time restrictions on presentation of petition for divorce. Secondly, it alters the position of women who are divorced abroad and, thirdly, it changes the law concerning financial arrangements after divorce.

When the Bill becomes law. you will no longer have to wait three years before being able to file for divorce. At present, unless you can prove that there has been exceptional hardship or depravity, you have to wait for three years before getting a divorce. You may, however, start proceedings for judicial separation within this time. Under the new Bill, this time limit is abolished in favour of an absolute ban on divorce within one year of marriage. You will still be able to file for a judicial separation within this time, but after one year it will not be necessary to provide evidence of exceptional hardship or depravity in order to file for divorce.

If you live in England or Wales and your marriage is ended by divorce proceedings abroad you will, under this Bill, be able to claim some financial compensation from your husband by taking out proceedings in this country, something that at present is impossible. The new provision should prevent the situation where a woman is divorced abroad without her knowledge and is not awarded any maintenance or share in the home.

The main part of the Bill is taken up with the financial arrangements made after divorce. The stated aim of the Bill is that priority should be given to the welfare of any children under eighteen years, but it does not specify what arrangements should be made to secure this. The main provisions are concerned with what should be taken into account when a court decides upon the level of maintenance to be awarded. The Bill removes the existing objective of putting both parties in the same financial position as if they had not divorced, and places more emphasis on other considerations. One of these is your earning capacity. This means that when assessing a level of maintenance, the court can look at what you are capable of earning in the future. The new Bill adds to this by saying that the court can take into account 'any increase in that capacity which it would, in the opinion of the court, be reasonable to expect a party of the marriage to take steps to acquire'. This means that not only can the court assume that you will be able to get a job with your existing skills, but it may predict that you are able to acquire new and different skills and then be able get a job. This extension of the existing power of the court to consider financial resources either you or your partner are likely to have in the future would appear to be mere speculation on the part of the judge. Your solicitor should make sure that the court is aware of the state of the job market and the discrimination against women by employers.

Another consideration for the court is the 'conduct' of the parties. This means that the court can take into account whether your husband has been violent or unreasonable in his behaviour, but it may also be used against you. In the existing law, conduct may be taken into account only after other factors have been considered and then only if the court feels it is 'just' to do so. The new Bill puts conduct on a par with the other factors to which the court must have 'particular regard'. This is less a change in the law than a change in emphasis, and could lead to more conflict during the proceedings.

A minor change introduced by this Bill concerns inheritance. At present you may decide with your husband not to benefit from his will, but the Bill gives the court the power to make that decision without your consent.

Finally, the Bill includes several provisions which allow the court to terminate maintenance payments either immediately or some time in the future. Under present law, it is quite common to get a nominal maintenance order which can be altered at a later date to a higher figure if circumstances change. The Matrimonial and Family Proceedings Bill makes it possible for the court to decide that there should be no continuing financial obligation. This arrangement is already quite common for couples who do not have children. It is clearly quite inappropriate in cases where there are children, but the Bill gives the court new powers to make such arrangements. You may not feel happy about having a nominal maintenance order, as it means some continued contact with your husband, but it means that, if necessary, you can go back to court if you need more money to support the children. Many women would prefer to be financially independent of their husbands, but given the lack of job opportunities for women and discrimination against women in the tax and social security systems, this is hard to achieve.

The court also has the power to use its discretion to limit a financial award in time. This means that you may be awarded some maintenance payments for a limited period of time. The Bill introduces a new section to the present legislation, instructing the court that the maintenance should last only as long as to prevent 'undue hardship'. The court may, at the same time as making an order ending financial obligation, direct that no further application for maintenance can be made in the future. This means that although your circumstances may change, you will not be able to start new proceedings for maintenance.

The effect of this new Bill is likely to be that women will be unable to get as much maintenance as the present laws allow. This is because the impetus for the Bill came from groups of (mainly) men who believe that there are many women who are financial drains on their ex-husbands and who live comfortably with no incentive to go out to work while the men struggle to support themselves and perhaps a new family. However, very few women are financially dependent upon maintenance: most have another source of income, which for many women is social security. The Bill promotes the idea that women should become self-sufficient as soon as possible after divorce. Some of the provisions are not intended to apply to women who have custody of children, but there is nothing in the Bill which prohibits their use in cases where there are children. Similarly, there is nothing in the Bill which confronts the problem of enforcement of maintenance orders.

INDEX